Mechanics and Meaning in Architecture

Mechanics and Meaning in
Architecture

Lance LaVine

University of Minnesota Press

Minneapolis • London

Copyright 2001 by the Regents of the University of Minnesota

Published by the University of Minnesota Press
111 Third Avenue South, Suite 290
Minneapolis, MN 55401-2520
http://www.upress.umn.edu

Library of Congress Cataloging-in-Publication Data

LaVine, Lance.
    Mechanics and meaning in architecture / Lance LaVine.
        p. cm.
    Includes bibliographical references and index.
    ISBN 0-8166-3476-9 (HC/J : alk. paper) — ISBN 0-8166-3477-7 (PB : alk. paper)
        1. Architecture and technology.   2. Architecture—Technological innovations.   I. Title.
    NA2543.T43 L38 2001
    720'.1'05—dc21

                                                                00-011808

Printed in the United States of America on acid-free paper

The University of Minnesota is an equal-opportunity educator and employer.

11 10 09 08 07 06 05 04 03 02 01   10 9 8 7 6 5 4 3 2 1

This book is dedicated to my father,
Eugene Howard La Vine, 1913–1999, and to my mother,
Lucille Gibbons La Vine, 1911–1998

Contents

Part II Mechanics and Meaning in Four Houses

Preface

The ideas that are presented in this book are the product of teaching in a school of architecture for nearly twenty years. Over the course of that experience, only on the rarest of occasions has a student exhibited a genuine interest in technology. The calculations required in structures, heat transfer, and illumination are normally considered to be irrelevant in design, if not damaging to the architectural imagination. The students who do find these issues interesting are those who are skilled in mathematics. Unfortunately, there seem to be no Christopher Wrens among them.

When I ask my students what I am sitting on during an informal part of a lecture, they inevitably reply in their educated intelligence that it is not the edge of a small table as it appears to be but rather an assembly of atoms and molecules that are predominately made up of empty space. When I point out to them that this is a fact that is not really in evidence to either one of us, they just shake their collective heads at my ignorance. No one answers that I am sitting on a table or even that I am sitting on an assembly of wood that we call a table. That would be to announce the obvious and the ignorance of the speaker in the process. When these same students are asked what a beam is later in their educational career there is an immediate strain to remember faint ideas of compression, tension, and bending moment. No one ever thinks of answering that the beam is the material shape that we see and touch. That again would seem to be to play the fool. Somehow we have corporately managed to reduce phenomena to terms that none of us fully comprehends. A table is a table and a beam is a beam in our commonly understood experience. What it means to be one of these things is too often bypassed in a common rush to the intelligence of abstraction. We no longer begin our deliberations concerning technology from a world of things that we know, but rather from a world of abstractions that constitute the way we think that we ought to consider these issues.

As I have watched this process throughout my years as a teacher, I have become aware that there is more to this split than meets the eye. Architects, beneath their special knowledge and skill, are apt representatives of the population at large. They too live in, feel, and think about the accommodations that have been built for them, as do all other people. Architects are just as moved by places of merit as are their architecturally less educated fellow citizens because architects bring the same basic equipment to the task of inhabitation as do their fellows. It is this commonality with other human beings, and not the inculcated values of the profession of architecture at any given time, that allows architects to understand the meaning of what it is to inhabit a place. The profession attempts to place this understanding outside the normal domain of other human beings because that is how architecture comes to have a special power in society. There is much to recommend the development of expertise by a profession, but expertise does not supersede the fact that architects experience the world in the same basic way that all other people do. This commonality of experience lies at the center of understanding the significance of architectural technology. If we can but tap that center, designers might come to learn something about their own craft that remains hidden from the engineer.

I, like all authors, have many people to thank for this opportunity. This book is dedicated to my mother and father because each contributed an ingredient to my personality that is essential to this production. From my mother came a love of making things and a respect for my hands. From my father came a love of ideas and a respect for my mind. William Porter of MIT was the person who first encouraged me to write this book. His insight into the problems of mechanics and meaning has been invaluable. My former dean, Harrison Fraker, has always been interested in this problem and so has brought more than the courteous support required of all administrators to this effort. Colleagues at the Society of Building Science Educators, including G. Z. Brown, Gail Braeger, Joel Loveland, Susan Ubelohde, Marietta Millet, Chris Benton, Jeff Cook, David Lee Smith, and Fuller Moore, have provided the incubating ground for many of the ideas of this book. But chief among those that should be thanked (but not held responsible for these ideas) is my friend and colleague Gunter Dittmar. Gunter and I were young teachers together at Minnesota seventeen years ago, when I was going to remake architectural theory in the form of operations research. All was to be explained in the wonderful rhetoric of my favorite graduate school instructor at the University of Pennsylvania, Russell Ackof. How much I have changed in this view is due in no small amount to the ongoing discussions I have had and the wisdom that I have received from Professor Dittmar. Professor Andrzej Piotrowski documented the mechanics of the technological systems of each building, supervised the construction of study models, photographed these models as a record of solar time, and provided ongoing insight and criticism concerning the ideas of this book. Harrison Fraker, Gunter Dittmar, Sharon Roe, Paul Tesar, Paul Clark, Carlos Naranjo, G. Z. Brown, and Tom Fisher served as readers during different phases of the development of the text. My thanks for their efforts and insights. My friend and colleague Simon Beason was similarly an ongoing source of both support and scholarly criticism. This book would never have come to fruition if it were not for the unusual investment of time and energy of Sharon Roe. The project was lying dormant when she resurrected it and me. Additional thanks are due to Andrew Vernooy of the University of Texas for his generous review of and comments on the text.

But as is so often the case in extended endeavors, it is my wife, Linda, who deserves my most heartfelt thanks. To live with a person who has been as preoccupied as I have in writing this book over the past three years is an act of generosity. To take an active interest in it, to read copy and offer comment, and to press for its completion lie far beyond the call of spousal duty. Thank you, Linda.

Introduction: The General Problem

Even the most pure forms of purpose are nourished by ideas—like formal transparency and graspability—which in fact are derived from artistic experience.
Theodor Adorno, "Functionalism Today"

When an architect sits down at a drawing board to begin work on a building design, his or her first thoughts are recorded in tentative sketches of plans and sections that will eventually develop into a design proposal. In these sketches are vague references to columns and walls that will support the weight of the building long before structural calculations define their exact position and size, to exterior walls as notions of enclosure long before their thermal properties are analyzed, and to openings for sunlight long before required footcandles of illumination have been established. These sketches are nascent architectural conceptions of technology. They begin to specify how a building will cope with the natural forces of gravity, climate, and sunlight before they are treated as issues of engineered calculation. Yet our culture tends not to think of these sketches as technological proposals because calculated performance has replaced architectural form as the primary definition of what is technological about buildings.

Privileging a definition of technology as measurable action over that of material form presents a problem for architecture. The calculations employed to measure technological performance in buildings are primarily the domain of engineering. The manipulations of the form of columns, walls, and windows of these buildings specified by drawings are primarily the domain of architecture. The calculations of the engineer cannot be seen to be either

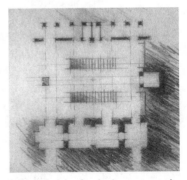

Initial sketch of a design proposal for a building.

inappropriate or unnecessary to an architectural understanding of technology, but neither do they, in and of themselves, provide an inclusive and satisfying definition of the role of technology in architectural design. Architectural drawings increase the scope of this definition by linking these technologies to human experience through the material forms they represent but sacrifice the authority that numbers bring to an understanding of technology in the process. The gulf between these two descriptions of the same phenomena is large. Most of us understand the actions of nature as numeric amount in one part of our minds while reserving another kind of thought to consider nature as value interpreted from form. We would no more think of merging these two modes of thought than we would consider placing the ideas concerning the structure of nature of Isaac Newton and William Shakespeare in the same category. One was a scientist, the other a poet. The differences in how each envisioned nature far outweigh any similarities that they might have in fostering a collective understanding of technology as the manipulation of that context.

Often this divided vision of technology is set aside through either indifference or ignorance of the problem it poses. We all behave, to some extent, as if inherent distinctions between conflicting visions of technology can largely be ignored because of the conveniences and privileges that these technologies have created in our lives. We act as if the differences suggested by numeric and visual representations of technology either are of little importance or have already been satisfactorily resolved, though there is little evidence to support this contention. Architecture, like the rest of us, is loath to question the character of a construct that has bequeathed so many gifts on it and on our society.

But as C. P. Snow has noted in *The Two Cultures*, this division of thought cannot be set aside lightly. Its roots are found in a general cultural disjunction between an abstract mathematical understanding of the natural world and a vision of that same world as an interpretation of the significance of our palpable existence within it. Snow speaks of this division as the gulf that has grown between the sciences and the humanities in our intellectual discourse. He claims that scientists and writers have ceased to converse because they lack a common vocabulary. Their consequent lack of communication precludes a full consideration of the richness of the human experience. Our understanding of nature is divided in two by the unrectified thought of these intellectual disciplines. One discusses nature as literal quantities that are the outcome of transactions of matter and energy but is mute concerning their value. The other speaks to the human significance of nature but is mute concerning its quantifiable operations. No bridge currently exists between these dichotomous visions.

Model of Finnish log farmhouse.

The following discussion seeks to illuminate the conditions necessary to understand architectural technology as both measured action and interpreted value by examining the oldest, most fundamental, and least machinelike of these technologies. This is an exploration of the qualities of walls, floors, and ceilings as weather envelopes, of columns and beams as structural frames, and of windows as transmitters of sunlight. These are the technological entities that architects manipulate in the procedures they call design, and these are the material entities that people inhabit in buildings.

Model of Charles Moore House in Orinda, California.

Four houses serve as the basis of this study. Two of these houses, the Villa Savoye and Tadao Ando's Wall House, are well known to architects, whereas the Finnish log farmhouse and Charles Moore's house at Orinda may be less well known. The reason for the selection of these buildings is not their fame among architects but the differences in attitude that each strikes in the use of technology. These differences serve to give substance to the quest for what is architectural about technology.

Model of the Wall House, by Tadao Ando.

This study will address the issue of the use of technology in design through the

Model of Villa Savoye, by Le Corbusier.

formal analysis of these buildings. There is some merit in attempting to understand the ideas of a discipline directly from the material form of the things that it creates. A formal analysis may seem to some to be a strange way to approach the problem of technology in buildings. I can only hope that the wisdom of this choice is borne out in the pages that follow. Although the liabilities of this kind of analysis in terms of technology are genuine, so are its potential benefits.

The general trajectory of this argument is that architecture has lost its own technological voice through the substitution of engineering's objective view for architecture's own, more metaphorical, understanding of technology's role in the design of buildings. This argument contends that:

- The use of technology in architecture is unique because it is habitational.
- As a technology of habitation, architecture's chief duty is to provide people with a place of residence in nature that makes that residence secure in all the ways that people require.
- Because people understand their condition symbolically as well as literally, architectural technology is required to give birth to an understanding of a symbolic nature as value, as well as of a literal nature of measurable action.
- Architectural technology proposes metaphorical ideas through technological forms that define nature to symbolically be a place of human residence.
- These metaphors emanate from a sensual understanding of nature as "felt force."

These conditions might be summarized by the following working definition of the role of technology in architectural design:

Architectural technology is the way in which human beings create metaphorical ideas that place them in nature through the manipulation of habitable form that redirects natural force.

This definition expands the role of technology in architectural design to include the possibility of the formation of metaphorical thought concerning natural force. This goal seeks not to displace but to supplement current conceptions of the use of technology in architectural design as calculated performance. Its objective is to begin to outline what is unique and essential about the use of technology in architectural design, to reclaim the world of natural force for meaningful interpretation in the design of buildings.

Part I

■

The Reconciliation of Mechanics and Meaning in Architectural Thought

1. A Technology of Habitation

When you understand all about the sun and all about the moon and all about the atmosphere and all about the rotation of the earth, you may still miss the radiance of the sunset.
Alfred North Whitehead, *Science and the Modern World*

Architectural technology is unique in that it contains us. We reside within these technologies rather than understanding them as separate and autonomous machines. The problem of what these technologies have come to mean as mechanisms of habitation has given them a particularly complex and intimate character. Because we live within them, these technologies are always charged with the responsibility of mediating between the physical characteristics of natural force and our thought about the significance of our own existence within these forces.

Two Definitions of Architectural Technology
Our sense of our existence in nature is presented to us by even the most mundane of architectural technologies. I like to sit next to my favorite window in my favorite chair while having my morning cup of coffee and browsing the headlines of the front page of the local newspaper. In the winter this is a special experience. I live in a northern climate where the ground is normally covered in a dense, granular snow for five months of the year. Winter mornings are cold and still in Minnesota, but the early sunlight of these days is often bright and radiant as it fills the room with an exuberant light. This is not a light that might be obtained in other parts of the year or in other rooms of the house. My window, chair, and room are only this way on clear winter mornings. A small part of my mind notices the winter morning sky when I awake to let me know if I can look forward to the light of my chair with confidence.

My winter morning ritual is not an unusual human event. We all experience the natural world through architectural technologies in much the same way. Everyone has a time of year or time of day

3

that they look forward to for similar reasons. Some travel to the south for winter vacations under the shade of a Mexican *palapa* (palm frond shelter), while others find that a north woods fireplace offers an equal measure of comfort. These experiences seem so normal to us, so commonplace, and so easily described. But the more deeply we examine them, the more elusive our understanding of them becomes. The more precise the language that is used to explain them, the more distant they become from our everyday lives. Why?

UNDERSTANDING ARCHITECTURAL TECHNOLOGIES AS HABITATION

We understand our habitation of these technologies in two very different ways. The first emanates directly from palpable human experiences like sitting next to my winter window. This experience has physical characteristics in that it modifies the way in which heat and light are allowed to enter and leave my room. Without this technology, I wouldn't be sitting in a bright—but ten-degree-below-zero—morning in my bathrobe. My body and mind easily register this physical difference. But there is more to inhabiting this technology than might be defined by the flow of heat and light. There is something about sitting at the boundary, being bathed in sunlight coming from a very cold outside while I'm warm inside, that makes this experience a little more special than it would be on a warm summer day. There is something reassuring about the exact placement of the chair in relation to the window. It seems to secure a place of safety in the face of near danger.

Though such distinctions may arise from the physical characteristics of my winter window, they are conceptually different from them. Each signifies an interpretation of the quality of my experience of a window as an idea that cannot be literally measured.

The second way of understanding this same architectural technology is through literal measurements. There are many ways to measure the quantitative characteristics of my window-lit room. I can measure the outside temperature, the inside temperature, the relative humidity, the rate at which heat is conducted, convected, and radiated from a warm inside to a cold outside, the amount of sunlight that is incident on the outside of the glass of the window, the amount of sunlight that passes through the glass, and the amount of light that is reflected from the surfaces of the room. I can build these and like measurements in ever greater detail until I have some confidence that my measurements accurately reflect

My window on a winter morning.

the dynamic physical characteristics of the environment that I am inhabiting.

MECHANICS AND MEANING IN AN ARCHITECTURAL TECHNOLOGY OF HABITATION

Measurement gives birth to thought about architectural technology as *mechanics*. Interpretation of human experience of the tangible form of these technologies gives birth to thought of architectural technology as *meaning*. Both are characteristics of the material form that primary architectural technologies assume in buildings as weather envelopes, structural frames, and windows.

Mechanics allow the way in which tasks are performed by building technologies to be quantified. Each wooden stud in the walls of my winter window room can be calculated to assume a portion of the structural loads that this wall must bear for the building to remain standing. An infrared photograph of the exterior wall and window of

5

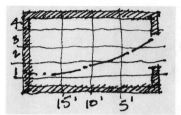

This isolux diagram of a window represents the percentage of outside illumination that might be expected to penetrate this space.

the room reveals the rate of flow of thermal energy from the inside to the exterior environment of the dwelling. An isolux diagram presents the quantitative distribution of light once it passes through the glass of the window into a room. Each is an empirical measurement of the tangible performance of an architectural technology as it reaches equilibrium with the natural force that it modifies.

Meaning seeks to establish the significance of these technologies to our existence as a function of their import and insight into the human condition. Architectural technologies physically modify nature so that people might bodily inhabit this context, but in so doing, they create another realm of ideas that seek to locate people mentally, emotionally, and spiritually within nature. Buildings cannot fail to make such statements because their technologies are housed in physical forms that reside in nature and, in turn, house us. We are symbolic as well as physical creatures. We cannot help attempting to interpret the symbolic significance of a physical world that surrounds us even as we are subject to its measurable consequence. There are no entities in this world that can simply be split into issues of measurable performance and those of interpreted symbolic meaning because our own experience of the world from which our buildings arise cannot be divided in this way. We live in the world of nature as a whole. We require a way to think of the technologies that allow us to do so that is parallel to our own sense of this existence.

The origin of the meaning of my winter window as a technology that locates me in nature is found in the particulars of my experience within it. The light that it brings into the room is "exuberant" rather than ordinary. My anticipation of this condition connotes a complex interweaving of sunlight as a natural force and a sense of human well-being. The window is said to create a bounded security within its surface as opposed to a boundless expanse of snow without. A particular chair in relation to a particular window cannot literally engender any such notions. Each is a way in which people place themselves in the natural world as an extension of the ideas that emanate from their sense of themselves. These interpretations of architectural technologies speak to an idea of habitation that subsumes the conditions of our existence—morning sunlight, coffee, newspaper—within the context of a nature of sensual, lived values. Place, domain, and boundary are ideas that are made possible by a symbolic generalization of these particular experiences within architectural technologies.

We know much about the character of nature as an extension of ideas that emanate from things that we make. If architectural technologies manifest both literal performance and symbolic meaning, then they must reflect an understanding of a natural context that also exhibits these characteristics. A quantitative understanding of architectural technologies is the province of engineering. If the character of nature is to be known through the interpretation of the qualities of architectural technologies, then they must be known as metaphoric extensions of the properties of these technologies. A metaphoric nature is the product of interpreting the tangible forms of architectural technologies to manifest intangible characteristics of the natural world that we reside within. This metaphoric interpretation of nature is the province of architectural design.

THE ENVELOPE, THE FRAME, AND THE WINDOW

The architectural technologies that serve to locate people in nature are as old as the act of building itself. The first architecture arose

The ideas necessary to understand architectural technology are no less complex than those required to understand the significance of the tangible forms of nature that surround us.

from the need to make places that could be warm when the climate was too cold, dry when the climate was too wet, and calm when the climate was too windy. In response to an inhospitable climate, people formed material into an enclosure that separated them from the weather. Maintaining this enclosure required that the constant pull of gravity of all objects to the surface of the earth be overcome. People created a second organization of material to hold the surfaces of the weather enclosure aloft. Once accomplished, the enclosure was dark. In separating inhabitants from the undesirable stresses of climate, the weather envelope of the building had inadvertently separated people from the light that allowed them to know where they were in relation to other things. Inhabitants of buildings cut holes in the surfaces that surrounded them to reestablish this connection. Thus the early development of shelter initiated the basic problems of the weather envelope as a response to climate, the structural frame as a response to gravity, and the window as a means to admit sunlight as technological issues in architecture.

UNDERSTANDING THROUGH USE

Our understanding of these habitational technologies has developed over the long history of their use. People first came to architectural-

The actual material form of a window inhabited by people is not the
direct outcome of its mechanics. These forms connote symbolic values,
such as the horizontal slit of the roof garden of Villa Savoye as
a metaphoric representation of the horizon.

ly understand natural forces as an extension of immediate sensual experience when they first attempted to manipulate these forces with the most primitive architectural technologies. Tools give explicit definition to natural force. The search for empirically effective architectural tools to keep the cold out and the envelope aloft, and to let the sunlight into buildings, allowed people to begin to take possession of natural force in a manner that might be manipulated mentally as well as physically.

Each use of an architectural technology fostered a character of natural force learned through its manipulation that was absent in an unmediated sensual definition of that force. The severity of winter was no longer as simple as it had once been. It became the thickness of the wall or an air space below a floor. Gravity was no longer what was heavy to lift but became the pattern of hierarchical order of the organization of wooden members of the roof of a farmhouse. Sunlight was not just the passing of the day but the way in which light brought distant objects into a relationship with things that were close at hand through a window.

Each of these tangible manipulations of a natural force with an architectural technology had the potential for symbolic distinctions built into its first use. The thickness of a wall in its most primitive form always separates. The origin of the mental construct "to separate" is probably due, in no small measure, to the act of building walls. The distinction "to order" was part of the most primitive roof structures. People had to decide whether the bigger piece sat on the smaller or vice versa. They had to decide how far apart big and small elements should be spaced to make a surface that could resist gravity over extended periods of time. A regular pattern of thickness and length of roof members emerged from this trial-and-error construction to become a foundation for the way in which people might imagine the concept of order. All that could be viewed from a window was thought to become a part of the belongings of a house. The distinction "domain" probably emanated from the extent of the landscape that could be seen from a particular vantage point such as that afforded by a window. These were hard-fought intellectual battles. What was learned from them was encoded in patterns of technological form that could transmit this knowledge. These patterns inherently contained undivided conceptions of mechanical utility and symbolic meaning about the natural world that serves as the context for human existence.

PURPOSES

Over this history of use, the most easily identified purpose of architectural technologies has been to allow human beings to survive in climates that were not hospitable. But the broad purpose of these technologies has never been limited to a simple matter of how they worked. Architectural technology has always been, at its heart, a more general way in which people have come to understand what characterizes the natural forces that form their context. Uses of these technologies extend the definition of the natural forces of climate, gravity, and sunlight from what might be sensed to what might be manipulated, and from what might be manipulated to conceptions of what such manipulations might mean. The empirical success of a manipulation causes an extension of what nature is thought to be. Failure of an architectural technology means not just that the technology was incorrectly conceived but that the natural phenomena that it was conceived to manipulate is not what it was assumed to be. Each technological manipulation of a natural force with a weather envelope, a structural frame, or an opening for sunlight thus creates a specific and literal manipulation of a force that is capable of generating more general vision of the character of the natural world that it modifies.

The primitive origins of these technologies may obscure their significance to us. Weather envelopes, structural frames, and openings for sunlight may seem to be trivial technical issues when compared with the wealth of mechanical invention that has occurred

The model of the underside of a wooden roof shows how progressively larger spanning members gather the weight of the surface of the roof to bring it to the walls in a pattern that we associate with order.

This window in a Chinese teahouse is placed
in such a way that the pagoda perched on
the side of a distant hill becomes framed as
a part of the domain of the room.

over the course of human history. No member of a sophisticated industrial society would think of a roof or a wall, a floor or beam, a
window or column as being in the vanguard of contemporary technological development. These societies see the propulsion and control systems of spacecraft, the possibility of gene splicing, and the
rapid increase in computer processing speed as truer measures of
technological progress. They imagine technology to be represented
by machines and the effectiveness of these machines in performing
tasks more quickly, with greater impacts, or with less resource as
the measure of the quality of this technology. Little wonder that
problems as mundane as keeping the cold out, standing upright, and
letting the sunlight in may appear archaic.

The weather envelope separates hospitable from inhospitable climates as it creates the symbolic distinction of inside and outside that is so central to architectural thought. Photograph by Simon Beason.

But architectural technology is a more complex phenomenon than it appears to be. This particular use of technology does not automatically replace old techniques with new, more efficient means to accomplish tasks, as some would profess. Architectural technology gathers up its history in its progress.

People are quite accustomed to this collapse of time when they employ these technologies. They see nothing unusual about standing on a wood floor that is technologically thousands of years old while regulating their interior climate with a thermostat that is the product of inventions of the past seventy-five years. It does not amaze them that they enjoy sitting in front of a fireplace while typ-

Technology exists in buildings as an indivisible confluence of symbolic meaning and utilitarian performance, here manifest in the corner detail of a Japanese Buddhist temple.

ing on a laptop computer. They are not taken aback by opening a window in the same world that builds supercolliders. Because of this collapse of technological time, the significance of these technologies might be better defined as an accumulation of human inventiveness rather than as a linear progression of measurable efficiency. The importance of these technologies is found not in when they were invented or how efficient they are but in what they have come to mean to a civilization.

The Problem of Mechanics and Meaning in an Architectural Technology of Habitation

CONDITIONS FOR AN ARCHITECTURAL TECHNOLOGY OF HABITATION

There are, then, not one but three conditions that are necessary to specify what is architectural about a habitational technology. The first of these is that architectural technologies do perform physical tasks. Natural force does exist as empirical fact. Transmissions of force that attend gravity, climate, and sunlight can be described through measurements. Nature does behave in a physically verifiable manner that might be codified and general-

ized as mathematical formulas. The reliability of these and like calculations has helped to establish the belief that the operations of the universe might be known through observation. Phenomena in the universe have been shown to exist in an orderly manner that allows mathematical predictions to be successful. Each discovery of an orderly phenomenon and its mathematical formulation can be added to an ever growing array of previous discoveries to form progressively more fundamental understandings of what underlie all physical manifestations of natural force. The efficacy of such proposals must always undergo the standard of predictive accuracy that modern science has established to gain acceptance by a larger community. The rigor of this proof is so powerful that it is often assumed to constitute the "truth" concerning the structure of nature.

The search for our place in the cosmos is a perennial architectural issue, as evidenced by the attitude struck by buildings from Stonehenge to the Salk Institute.

The second of these conditions is the need for a human abstraction to be formulated, which subsumes these mechanical facts in a more general notion of the significance of our existence in nature. Physical measurement is not synonymous with the ways in which human beings understand their natural context. To understand natural phenomena as numerical quantification alone is to reduce nature to ideas of mechanics independent of other human intelligence and its outcomes as nonmathematical thought. But people experience the natural world through architectural technologies with all their senses. Their explanations of these sensations arise from the complexities of being human. They need to define their context at a parallel level of complexity to belong within it. People's definitions of the natural world thus tend to be extensions of the wholeness of their own existence.

The third condition is the need to develop a formal metaphor for this human abstraction of domain that allows intangible abstractions to be glimpsed through the characteristics of their tangible analogues. Values that grow out of the richness of human experience, such as my fondness for early-morning winter sunlight, cannot be known literally, as can mechanics. They are values that constitute human interpretations of our condition and hence need to be explained in other than literal terms: they must be explored metaphorically. Technological form in architecture creates metaphoric thought about how we belong within a natural context as a function of its significance to us.

THE ISSUE

The issue for architecture is not that a metaphoric world needs to subjugate a mechanical conception of nature or vice versa. It is rather that the relationship between the two needs to be understood and valued. Understanding nature as mechanics and as meaning is a problem that confronts every human being. We live in our full sense of how we exist in the world. This sense cannot be arbitrarily truncated to focus on issues and modes of thought that can be described with mathematical accuracy because we do not think all of our significant thoughts as the outcome of numbers. We understand the world through the agencies of touch, sight, hearing, and smell, powerful senses that defy exact quantification. We think of our place in the world in terms such as separation, order, and domain that do not have mathematical analogues. The "exuberant" sunlight of my winter window or the sense of adventure that emanates from being next to a thin, transparent boundary are more-than-sufficient reminders that architectural technologies are constituted of more than their mechanics.

Yet we also live in a world where objects fall to the earth at a mathematically predictable rate, where heat passes from regions of higher to lower energy in conformance with numerical formulas, and where the amount of light reflected from a surface can be measured with great accuracy. My ability to be adjacent to a cold outdoor climate while wearing a bathrobe testifies to the mechanical importance of a window as an architectural technology. To suggest that one of these two ways of knowing nature should be subjugated to the other in architectural technology is absurd. It solves the problem of the way in which human beings understand their circumstances by ignoring major components of how people think and feel.

THE PROBLEM OF RECONCILIATION

If we agree that the metaphoric meaning of my experience of a winter morning window and the measurement of its mechanics are both necessary to understanding it as a technology, then architecture is left with a difficult problem. How do these two understandings of a common phenomenon fit together? What might be the relationship between a natural world that is measured and calculated and one that is felt and interpreted to manifest human value that is unmeasurable? How might architects understand these two worlds of nature in a way that allows them to move from one to the other in hopes of revealing the full measure of the richness that human occupation of the natural world might imply?

This, then, is the problem that architecture faces when it proposes the use of habitational technologies in buildings. In the small and ordinary illustration of my morning window lie the seeds of what makes understanding these technologies a rich, complex, and difficult architectural construct. This window produces both a literal and a metaphorical understanding of the nature that we inhabit. Portions of this understanding cannot be mathematically measured. As quality rather than quantity, they must be understood through inference. They are inexorably linked to the physical actions of nature, but the forces that govern the actions, and thus the characteristics of that nature, are invisible to the human mind in and of themselves. If they constitute a nature that can be known in everyday

15

existence, they must be known through phenomena that exhibit the qualities that are thought to characterize the natural world.

This dual responsibility of technology constitutes a dilemma for architectural thought. Architects cannot do without the powerful view of technology presented by mechanics because buildings do need to work in an empirical nature. This viewpoint is such a compelling advocate for its own kind of contribution to design that it is often assumed to be the sum of what constitutes architectural technology. But the procedures that constitute architectural design consider these technologies in a different way: they are represented as forms that create ideas concerning the human significance of the nature that we inhabit. Such forms may contain the roots of numerical analysis, but how they might do so is less clear than is the range of symbolic ideas that they suggest. These two visions of architectural technology now sit in an uneasy relationship to each other. There currently exists no convincing bridge between them as characterizations of the same events.

2. Architecture's Loss of a Distinct Technological Voice

Meanwhile the mind, from pleasure less,
Withdraws into its happiness;
The mind, that ocean where each kind
Does straight its own resemblance find;
Yet it creates, transcending these,
Far other worlds and other seas;
Annihilating all that's made
To a green thought in a green shade.
Andrew Marvell, "The Garden"

If architecture is to give explicit voice to a technology of habitation that includes both metaphoric meaning and measured mechanics, then it will need to understand the origins of this voice as consistent with its disciplinary constructs and values. This voice, rarely clearly enunciated, has been confused and suppressed by the emergence of engineering as a powerful building profession. In response to engineering's increasing authority over matters of the use of technology in buildings, architects have attempted to appropriate that discipline's constructs as their own. The outcome is a confusion of technological responsibility. The architectural problem inherent in this confusion is not to be found in engineering. Engineers continue to admirably develop their own technological craft. The problem lies, rather, in architecture's inability to define the unique contribution that it might make to the use of technology in buildings.

Engineering and Architectural Technology

THE RISE OF ENGINEERING AS A BUILDING PROFESSION

In the mid-nineteenth century, engineers came to a new prominence in the building professions. The Crystal Palace led a series of civic projects that placed engineers in positions of technological leadership. The use of iron and steel, first in railroad bridges and later in

The Crystal Palace, designed by the botanist
Joseph Paxton, was constructed in six months
from modular cast- and wrought-iron structural
elements bolted together to receive thousands of
pieces of glass. Etching courtesy of Phaidon Press.

building frames, was led by engineers whose values were far more
akin to those of a flowering capitalism than were those of the architectural profession of the time. Issues of heat and ventilation were
likewise pushed forward by professions other than architecture. The
British medical establishment led in a search for healthier air to
breathe than was available to typical eighteenth-century urban dwell-
ers. A series of inventors, including Franklin and Rumford, explored
more efficient ways of converting fuel to usable heat to climatize
buildings. Edison led the development of the electric light in 1879
and in the means to generate and distribute electricity to power
these lightbulbs soon thereafter. Each of these was a measured re-

sponse to a problem that might be quantitatively defined. Industrial air was full of measurable particulates that cause diseases. Fireplaces were extremely inefficient sources of heat. And electric light produced illumination without the residue of combustion that typified its gas predecessor.

The professions that took up these problems had a tradition of empirical problem solving. As advocates of a similar perspective, engineers quickly became forceful voices in the development of design ethics. This newfound power is made clear in descriptions of engineers as "functional professionals," "functional intellectuals," and "professional executives" in Raymond Merritt's *Engineering in American Society, 1850–1875*. What could possibly be more appealing to late-nineteenth-century society than a design profession that intelligently followed the dictates of utilitarianism in providing low-cost solutions to the myriad of practical building problems that confronted the era? A reputation for conscientiously managing the construction of projects did little to tarnish the societal image of the engineer as a "rational" design expert. The following quotation from Merritt's book suggests the range and depth of authority that the engineering profession had assumed in an era that was beginning to feel the muscular impacts of the industrial revolution.

> As their profession achieved the authority and freedom physically to transform American society, some engineers developed a fanciful vision of the emerging urban world, a new era that John A. Roebling termed a "Social Eden." Roebling based his utopia on the hope that the physical transformation engineers were bringing about would make possible the fulfillment of man's spiritual need for order, unity, and peace, ideals that shine through all of his writings. Technology would form the basis of this new community and restore a respect for truth, industry, economy, and social service. (136–37)

If the word *fanciful* is set aside as the historian's commentary rather than the engineer's objective, it suggests the extremely ambitious program of nineteenth-century engineering values and expertise. What might have been considered utilitarian means by a culture were now being proposed by this able group of entrepreneurs as the basis of the deepest values of society. Order, unity, peace, truth, and social service became the logical outcomes of the rational paradigms of engineering in this visionary world. The power of the utilitarian and functionalist logic that characterizes engineering was now to be applied to all the activities of a society to generate a functional utopia. It is a wonder, given the breadth and depth of this vision, that the engineering profession did not take over the management of the production of the constructed environment altogether.

OVERLAYING ENGINEERING TENETS ON ARCHITECTURAL THOUGHT

Nineteenth-century architecture took an ambivalent stance toward this intrusion. Both sides of the issue were reflected in major texts of the time. John Ruskin's *Seven Lamps of Architecture* warned that the advent of the industrial revolution signaled a great danger to architecture. His vision of buildings as anchored deeply in historical traditions was threatened by the utilitarian stance of the engineers of this new era. In reply to this threat, Ruskin developed a conception of beauty clearly differentiated from that of utility. Beauty could only begin where utility ended in this construct in an architecture that aspired to the higher aims of fine art.

Horatio Greenough, writing at approximately the same time, saw this issue from the opposite perspective. He suspected the nineteenth-century propensity for the appropriation of historic styles to be an empty and superficial gesture in the face of new possibilities and new attitudes propelled by the industrial revolution. His proposal that buildings be designed to find their own functional expression was a kind of architectural Darwinism. Greenough's claim that lions and giraffes, while dissimilar in form, were both beautiful because their shape was "fit to purpose" grounded a logic of functionalism in architecture that envisioned utility to be inseparable from beauty in buildings.

By the 1920s, engineering values that had long been held by a utilitarian commercial bourgeoisie were formally adopted by architecture as a mainstay of the avant-garde. The new technology became the subject of a broad range of manifestos written by architects at the beginning of the century. Ocean liners and automobiles, which were made honorific in Le Corbusier's *Towards a New Architecture*, had already been accepted by a late-nineteenth-century culture recognizing that technology was the wave of the future and that this wave would be led by engineers and scientists.

The Bauhaus attempted to incorporate engineering values in architecture in its notion of modernism. The educational program of this institution included attention to industrial means of production, the materials of the new age, and the special kinds of issues

In the Hong Kong Bank by Norman Foster, the structural system of
the building as industrial scaffold becomes the dominant generator
of the building's formal composition.

that faced industrial cultures. It attempted to legitimize functional
logic that lay at the core of engineering in architecture by making
the goals of that discipline appear to be coincident with its own.
The difference was that in the Bauhaus manifesto, utility was to be
expressed as architectural form instead of calculated with numbers.
Though the designs for buildings that emerged from this platform
often looked as if they worked at the expense of actually performing
empirical tasks well, the ground of their design ethic was not in
question. Architecture had assumed Greenough's stance with regard
to utility and joined engineers as the new guardians of "fitness to
purpose." The impact of this stance and its relation to technology
would reverberate throughout the modern movement across both
cultures and time. It is still felt by a global profession today.

This overlay of engineering values on the architectural use of
technology is reflected in the way in which many architectural critics assume this issue should be treated in the design of buildings.
Reyner Banham begins his discussion of the architect Le Corbusier
in *The Architecture of the Well-Tempered Environment* in a manner
that leaves little doubt as to his allegiances in this regard.

> Even though the implicit and explicit premises of his [Le Corbu-
> sier's] writings lay him open to more damaging attack, he was

probably no worse than the rest of his generation, the rest of the connection who, under the guise of the official establishment of the Congress Internationale d'Architecture Moderne, became the official establishment of architecture in our time. The whole generation was doubly a victim; firstly of an inability of its apologists and friendly critics to see architecture as any more than a culture problem, riding upon a conventional view of function that had not been related to twentieth-century needs; and secondly of its own (apparently willing) submission to a body of theory more than half a century behind the capabilities of technology, still preoccupied with problems—such as the use of metal and glass in architecture—that had been propounded by the generation of Sir Joseph Paxton and Hector Horeau in the 1850's, and so effectively solved by those mid-Victorian masters that the practical results were common knowledge for those, like Paul Scheerbart, who cared to seek them out at first hand. (143)

There is little sense in this critique that the values of technology in the early works of modern architecture should not be derived from utilitarian notions of technology as a tool that performed a task effectively. Ideas outside this framework of utilitarian effectiveness were simply considered to be wrongheaded. The technological ethics of engineering are applied so unquestioningly to the problem of architectural design in this contention that they would appear to have no competitors. But behind this seeming confidence lay a suspicion that there were major differences in the ways that architecture and engineering viewed technology. This doubt was manifest in the periodic and perpetual call for the integration of the two disciplines.

Modern architecture's repeated failures to accomplish Roebling's romanticized outcomes by adopting a technological design ethic grounded in engineering should have suggested that there was something more wrong with this contention than might be easily mended. Much of the reason for these failures might be traced to architecture's misunderstanding of its own versus engineering's attitudes toward design. A closer examination of the values that propel the design efforts of the two disciplines reveals major differences in the foundations of their technological thought.

A Case in Point

The mid-1970s were a productive era in the development of technologies to passively heat buildings. These technologies were pri-

Oroborous, a research project of the University of Minnesota, was designed to be heated with solar energy and electrified by a windmill. A clivus multrum processed human waste into the soil.

marily the result of trial-and-error field experiments, but much of the protocol needed to calculate the performance of passive solar systems had been codified by Douglas Balcomb and others of Los Alamos Laboratories by the late 1970s. The result was that both a menu of passive heating and cooling strategies and the requisite mathematical algorithms to predict their performance were available to architects in the 1980s. At the time, the technologically progressive in architectural education thought it imperative to incorporate these thermal building strategies in architectural education. A competition was held to determine how this integration of calculable solar gains might most effectively be incorporated in the curriculum of schools of architecture. The following experiments are taken from attempts to do so.

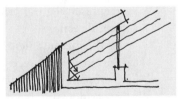

The knowledge empirically gained in projects such as Oroborous was transferred to students and practitioners in diagrams such as this one, which attempts to maximize the amount of heat gain of the building.

The first experiment proposed that the key to integrating this technical information into design thought and procedures

23

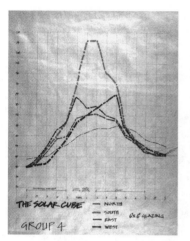

THE SOLAR CUBE — NORTH
GROUP 4 — SOUTH 6×6 GLAZING
— EAST
— WEST

This graph records the performance of a cube with a six-by-six-inch opening on one side. This outcome is a classic demonstration of the availability of solar energy by orientation.

was an acquisition of an empirical understanding of the thermal impacts of accepting visible sunlight into a space by designers. An exercise was generated to make these impacts measurable. Eight four-person student teams constructed four one-foot cubes with identical openings of a specified size on one of their sides. These cubes were made of one-inch-thick Styrofoam, and their openings were covered with cellophane. On a cold, clear December morning, the cubes were placed in an open athletic field adjacent to the school, each facing a different cardinal direction. Each cube contained a dry-bulb thermometer, and a fifth thermometer was placed near the cubes, but not in the sun or wind, to record ambient temperatures. Temperatures inside each cube and of the external thermometer were monitored and recorded each hour from 8 A.M. to 5 P.M. The results of this experiment were transferred to large graphs that placed the findings of each team concerning the amount of solar gain achieved by north, east, south, and west facing openings in a uniform format. Outcomes were compared and discussed, with participating students and studio critics noting the difference in temperature profiles of the cube as representing the principles of solar gains of windows facing different directions.

The measurements of the heat produced by the sun in the cubes were extremely successful. Students were easily able to conduct the experiment and to unambiguously document solar gains. Comparative results stimulated a lively discussion in the class review of the comparative results of the experiment, and considerable interest in energy issues seemed to be generated in students by making what for many was a vague principle into a tangible phenomenon.

What happened, then, in the translation of these empirical findings into design? Evaluation of final building designs that followed the completion of this solar experiment yielded no perceivable design impacts of the exercise. Window size and placement in the designs of students who participated in this exercise did not vary in

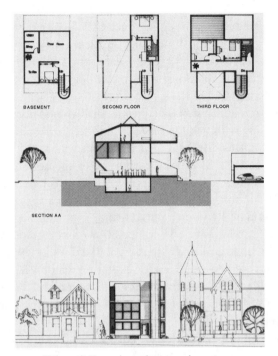

BASEMENT   SECOND FLOOR   THIRD FLOOR

SECTION AA

Although the solar cube experiment was
enlightening, it had no impact on the succeeding
design exercise.

any significant manner from those of a control group who designed the same structure without the benefit of the solar cube exercise. Apparently palpable demonstration of an empirical principle was not tantamount to implementation of that principle in design.

A second exercise taught later in the same design studio took up this issue, in a much different manner. Instead of attempting to premise design constructs on the measured impacts of insulation on an interior space, the window that was architecturally responsible for this transaction was defined to be "a precious object." The qualitative "preciousness" of the window was suggested by noting that it is the only architectural element that does not occur in the dwellings of animals and hence represents a uniquely human design act. Information provided to the students to reinforce the idea that the architectural creation of a window is a design decision not to be taken lightly discussed windows as the mediator of energy flows in and out of buildings, as the progenitor of architectural space, and as a venerable tradition in buildings such as igloos, pueblos, Chinese courtyard houses, English manor houses, the Crystal Palace, the Wainwright Building, the Lever Building, the Douglas House, and the Linz Café. The relationship of technology, human values, and design was compared in these discussions to convey an overview of both utilitarian and symbolic concerns that architecture has developed in dealing with windows as a seminal act of design.

Following this discussion, each student was asked to define in painting or collage the quality of light he or she desired in a space that housed a table and two chairs. The times selected for documentation of this luminescent quality were 9 A.M. on a spring day, noon on a summer day, 4 P.M. on a fall day, and 10 A.M. during the winter. The drawings, paintings, and compositions that resulted were presented by their authors and discussed by the class as a whole. These paintings then served as a basis for exploring window-wall relationships in study models and finally served as an integral part of the design exercise, which dealt with the building envelope as "a skin thick with issues."

The design impact of this exercise was substantial in thought, process, and product. Students found the idea of "the precious window" interesting enough to discuss among themselves, and the painting exercise was effective as a vague but somehow inviting way to envision solar space as evidenced in the products of their work. This impact was often carried through from study models into actual building design.

The strength of this exercise was its ability to generate qualifiable energy constructs in architecture. The paintings served as a vehicle for students both to explore the impacts of sunlight on space and to discuss the thermal costs of that sunlight. The method of exploration, models and paintings, allowed energy concerns to enter the conceptual deliberations of the project in a less determinate manner than that of calculations and hence in a way that was more open to conjecture than the

This student watercolor painting served as a luminescent provocateur for subsequent design work.

numerical evaluations of the first exercise. This level of openness to interpretation appeared to be more congruent with the architectural process for considering fundamental symbolic, contextual, and functional issues during the conceptual phases of design than were the measurements of the first exercise. Coding the concept in metaphorical terms as "the precious window" created an idea that was compatible with other value statements that initiated design proposals. Such phrases seem appropriate to the level of thought flexibility required at the conceptual levels of design. The slogan "the precious window" continued to appear throughout the remainder of the year, indicating that students had internalized the general notion of the importance of windows in design.

Certainly these two experiments pose a provocative foundation from which the incorporation of engineering information in architectural thought might be more clearly understood. The contention that the experiments were conducted with students and thus are not applicable to more mature design procedures would not be borne out by an examination of common architectural practice of

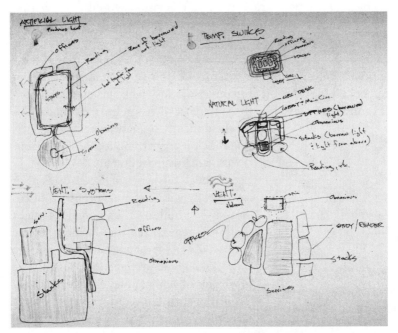

Each of these developmental drawings reveals conceptual impacts of natural sunlight both as light and as heat on the organizations of rooms within a plan.

technological design. The calculations of engineers requisite to completing building construction documents succeed rather than preceed most traditional architectural designs. Few architects base their design decisions on anything but the most primitive of numerical concerns for the technologies that they employ. Their decision-making procedures with regard to technological issues are much more akin to that put forward by "the precious window" than to the information provided by the solar cube.

While it might be argued that this inability to incorporate empirical measurement more directly into making design decisions is exactly what is wrong with architectural design as a decision-making process, the outcomes of these two experiments might just as convincingly be treated as the basis for understanding the differences between engineering and architectural visions of technology. Those who argue the former would contend that the very rise to prominence of engineers in the building professions in the nineteenth century was, in fact, premised on architecture's decision not to take up technical issues with a scientific rigor that would come to be characterized as "rational thought" concerning the use of technology. Those who argue the latter position would counter that such a wholehearted incorporation of engineering logic in architecture points toward the demise of the discipline's broad vision of the value of buildings. They would contend that the importance of these experiments was not to demean an empirical vision of nature but rather to point out the different ways in which this empirical context might be viewed. In this difference of vision lies the foundations of the difficulty of incorporating engineering thought concerning technology directly into architectural design.

Though this series of experiments dealt specifically with technical problems of energy use in buildings, its outcomes might be easily generalized to all aspects of the current use and thought concerning the role of technology in architectural design. The problems of sunlight and gravity may vary from those of climate in detail, but the general outline of the way in which they are currently understood in architecture is identical to those of climate. It makes little

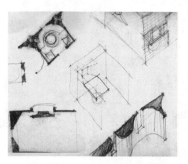

These conceptual sketches investigate the possible meaning of a window in a wall.

difference if it is the flow of British thermal units, the flow of foot pounds, or the level of measured foot-candles on a surface. In each case, quantities of natural force are entered in algorithms that profess to predict the performance of these technological systems. The outcome of each is premised on the contention that the goodness of an architectural technology might be determined by the quantification of its effectiveness as it redirects the natural forces of gravity, climate, and sunlight. The basic framework of these contentions and procedures holds true no matter what the particulars are of the technological issue being considered.

Distinctions That Arise from This Ground

The following major distinctions between architecture and engineering as modes of technological design thought might be understood in the analysis of these two exercises.

SPACE VIEWED AS OBJECT VERSUS THE SPACE OF INHABITATION

Engineering conceptually views space from without; architecture conceptually views space from within. To an engineer, a construction is an assembly of objects. The critical aspect of these objects is the way in which they transfer forces one to the other. If the totality of a construction cannot be seen by an engineer from outside of this assembly, he or she will not be in the privileged position to see and understand the complete net of force transactions that allow the construction to function effectively. This standing outside in order to understand the complete system of mechanical interchanges that constitute a construction's ability to perform a task is, in large measure, a creation of modern science. Before the use of scientific methods in building technologies, engineers depended on their experience and a general awareness of how materials responded to force to design structures. The presence of the engineer in the system was the presence of his or her total experience and values, so that nonquantifiable issues of expression in the design of structures often crept into the process of making quantifiable decisions under the guise of mechanical efficiency.

In the final analysis, however, all engineering looks for members of an organization of parts to do their job effectively. That is why the engineering emphasis on the evaluation of these structures has always been a matter of what was bigger, longer, faster, or taller. Success is found in the mechanical efficiency of the whole.

Accomplishing more with less has always been the goal of engineering. Understanding this efficiency is a matter of understanding all the parts and their relationships at once. Seeing all these relationships simultaneously requires a privileged view from outside the system.

The architectural view of space proves to be of a very different conceptual character from that of engineering. It is true that architects often begin to investigate the organization of a building in plan and that the plan of a building is a view of space from without. The difference between this view and that of engineering, however, is that the spaces organized by architects are seen as being populated by human beings rather than by forces. The plan as an overview contains a vision of space that people might inhabit as its core. A reciprocal relationship is established in these drawings between the way in which space has been experienced in existing structures and the way in which it will be experienced in the building being planned. This tie between the abstraction of the drawing and the realm of human experience means that this space is being considered in ways that include all the senses that define the inhabitation of space. This space is seen, but it is also felt, heard, smelled, and touched. It is never experienced by the inhabitant from the privileged objective point of view from without but is sensed only from within as the experience of a single instant of time. Visions of the whole must be visions of memory carried along with exposure to each new occupation of space. The integration of the whole must occur in the human mind, where it is susceptible to being reshaped by the values of the collected experiences of the inhabitant. The transaction between the conception of architectural space and the message that is received by building inhabitants is fundamentally undependable because these transactions are given to all the complexity that any human existence in its totality suggests. What is conveyed by the view of space from within is thus, by nature, a partial view of the whole that is experienced in specific places at specific times, with all the inhabitants' senses, all the collected ways they have experienced space over the course of their existence, and all the ways in which they have thought about these spaces.

The solar cube experiment proposed an engineer's view of space from without. Though these cubes possessed an interior, it was populated only by thermodynamic interchanges. The significance of this exercise was that designers could envision the complexities of the

The plan of Central Beheer, by Herman Hertzberger, is the blueprint of an idea of how many employees might inhabit this space.

sun as a source of energy, of the window as a means to transmit that energy, and of the interior surfaces of the cube as a means to convert visible light into heat as a single system of interlocked actions and reactions. The view of space put forward in the second exercise was the architect's vision of space from within. In their paintings, designers offered their attitudes toward being housed in sunlight as representative of a broader population's general attitude toward illumination. The power of sunlight to modify human experience in a range of ways as felt in the luminescent conditions proposed by each painting suggests a condition central to the idea of inhabitation.

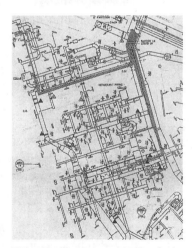

This plan illustrates a mechanical engineer's vision of a space like that of Central Beheer.

There is, then, a large gulf between an engineering view of the space and an architectural view of the same at the outset. This difference does not lend itself to integration simply because its point of departure is so different. The experience of space from within is an analogue of the complexity of human existence. It is fraught with all the perils and rewards that this complexity can deliver. The view from without attempts to reduce a portion of this complexity to a manageable set of understandable interchanges. What it loses in being an accurate analogue of human experience, it gains in the ability to predict and control the variables that it does focus on. The division between these two views of space constitutes a large obstacle to integrating the two disciplines.

NUMERICAL AND FORMAL SYMBOLS

The symbols that each discipline uses to manipulate ideas serve to widen this division. Engineers use numbers to give quantifiable dimension to the phenomena that they are attempting to manipulate. Architects draw and build models of their projects. The kinds of symbols that a discipline uses define both the kinds of ideas that it can deal with effectively and those that it cannot. The numbers of engineers are intended to mean one thing and one thing only. A dead load of 20 pounds per square foot is not intended to be interpreted as 19 or as 21 pounds, but only as 20 pounds per square foot. Thermal transfers and illumination are no different. A heat loss specified in Btus may not prove to be exactly accurate in field measurements, but it is intended to be. In the ideal world of an electrical engineer, illumination levels would be exactly reflected in lighting performance. The duty of a number is to convey an idea that is an exact analogue of its symbol. Numbers are the way in which people attempt to know with certainty portions of the world that might be known through this kind of symbol. The value of numbers used by the various engineers who help to design buildings is to express technological performance in buildings without equivocation. They reduce the world of technological ideas to those that can be conceived, manipulated, and conveyed with universal mathematical certainty.

What, then, of the symbols manipulated by architects? Might they also be specified as measurable quantity that can be accurately conveyed by number? A line of a drawing has length; a piece of model building material has surface area; the outcome of a design can be measured as volume. Should we therefore assume that architects are manipulating the same symbol system that is being manipulated by engineers, albeit to somewhat different ends? The heart of this distinction lies in the kinds of ideas expressed by these symbols and not in the similarities of a few of their characteristics. Architectural symbols denote amount as an outcome of the pursuit of other kinds of ideas, but not as the central objective of their formulation. The lines of an architect's drawing or the surface of a modeling material gain their significance only in the context of all the other lines or all the other surfaces that have been assembled in the design. They do not convey an inherent and inviolate meaning as do numbers but rather convey a meaning that depends on the context in which they are placed.

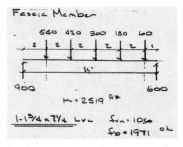

Engineers use numbers to specify the amount of energy that architectural technologies transport or modify. These calculations specify the loading conditions of a beam as a means to specify its size.

The goal of formal symbols is not to ascertain with universal certainty independent of context but to reveal the human significance of phenomena within a specific context. They are therefore the product of a particular kind of interchange that human beings have with their surroundings. This interchange is characterized not by literal amount but rather by an interpretation of insights that might arise from a figural understanding of the world.

The differences in the kinds of information and the outcomes of

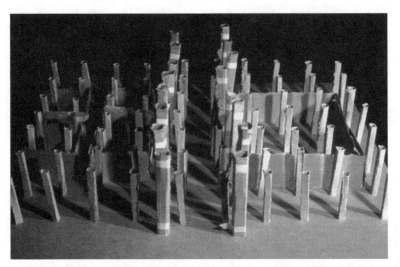

This model investigates the relationship of columns that will propel the design of a library. Structural calculation by David McDonald of Mattson McDonald Consulting Engineers.

the energy in design experiments described earlier become more clear in light of a definition of the symbols that designers were being asked to use interchangeably. The experiments that had numerical outputs succeeded as physics experiments because that's exactly what they were. These numbers were unavailable to interpretation as form because as physics experiments, they were coded in a symbol system designed to eliminate any range of ideas that might be interpreted from them. Encoding this same information in the words "the precious window" conversely eliminated the exactitude with which the numbers defined the phenomena of heat or light transmission and in so doing facilitated a formal discussion of the role of daylight in design. Numbers contained no memory of cold winter nights or crisp, crystalline winter days that are captured in sayings like "the precious window." The complexity of the value exchange of light for heat encoded in "the precious window" was unavailable to the information provided by physics experiments. How warm a solar-heated space might become was a matter of absolute measurement in the physics experiments but was a matter of the relative values of touch and sight in which each gave a special experiential meaning to the other in "the precious window." That the numbers of the first exercise and the paintings of the second were used to describe a common set of natural forces and the way in which these forces are modified by architecture does not do away with the differences in the ideas that these symbols are able to express.

APPLIED PRINCIPLE VERSUS EMERGENT INSIGHT

It is clear from distinctions inherent in both the view of space and the use of symbols that architects and engineers must think about the creation of designs for buildings in different ways. They do. Engineers conceive of designs as the application of principles that are encoded in rules that specify how natural forces behave under particular conditions. Architects are uncertain of the structure of ideas that are significant to a design at the outset of their work and use the process of design as an investigation into the relative significance of a number of possible issues in a project. To the engineer, the architect's decision-making process appears to be a labyrinth of personal interpretations and preferences. To the architect, the decision-making process of the engineer appears to be a rote system of problem solving that can only deal with a limited range of issues that must be framed in terms that lend themselves to the engineer's method rather than to the full complexity of an issue of design as an analogue of human experience. To a large extent, both critiques are correct. Engineers do define problems in quantifiable terms that conform to the ideas that their discipline is able to manipulate. They do apply either empirically or scientifically derived rules to this converted data to arrive at conclusions concerning the performance of materials under the stress of natural forces. They do see themselves, in the main, as problem solvers of issues that have already been specified by an architect's design for a building rather than as the generators of that design. Conversely, architects see their personal taste and insight into a problem as a legitimate grounds for initiating a solution. The kind of rules that they have developed to condition this search are far less explicit and yield far less certain results than do those of the engineer. Because architects are manipulating formal rather than numerical symbols in this search, the meaning of all that has gone before is subject to change with the addition of a singe line of drawing or the insertion of a single piece of modeling material. Architects build up the logic of their conclusions by adding and deleting formal symbols until they have reached a solution that is primarily a function of their judgment. Verifying the quality of these decisions can only come in the form of the concurrence of other judgments. Engineers apply principles that have been agreed to before the process of design is initiated; architects build up a case of relative decisions whose rightness can be judged only at the completion of design.

The solar cube experiment yielded factual data that would appeal to the thought processes of engineers. The paintings of the second exercise yielded vague notions of the possible significance of sunlight in a space that might be built into progressively richer conceptions of what that sunlight might come to mean to occupants of that space. This possibility is grist for the mill of architectural thought. The solar cube experiment complies with the rules of thermodynamics. The paintings offer opportunities for continued interpretation in search of the significance of sunlight in creating ideas of place.

SINGLE TRUTHS VERSUS FIGURAL ISSUES OF INHABITATION

These methods are directed toward two different kinds of outcomes by these two professions. In a perfect world of engineering there would be only one right answer to a technological problem. That answer could be derived from a perfect understanding of the forces of nature and the limits of material or energy in modifying that force. Conceptually there is only one right answer to the question of how to span a space with the minimum amount of material or how a space can be heated or cooled using the least amount of energy. The ability to reach this answer in reality may be frustrated by an imperfect knowledge of natural force, of the mechanical characteristics of materials, of different forms of energy and their transformation, of the vagaries of actual rather than theoretical construction processes, or of the differences in the actual versus intended uses of a building. Yet beneath these layers of unpredictability, which are tolerated but not admired by engineers, lies the secret desire for a uniform world that conforms exactly to prediction. That is why the longest, tallest, fastest, and biggest have so much more meaning to an engineer than to an architect. It is in these moments of extension of limits that the true characteristics of natural forces and the true mechanical limits of building materials or energies become evident. The goodness of an engineering solution to a problem is always measured in its ability to test the mechanical limits of a problem. Elegance is a measure of how close the solution comes to approximating the least material or energy required to modify the most natural force.

The "truths" of architectural thought revolve around the power of constructed environments to reveal the ideas that make our place on the earth knowable in all the terms that constitute human thought, as in the Reoninji Rock Garden in Kyoto.

Long spans such as those of the Golden Gate Bridge are meaningful to
engineers because they approach the limits of performance of a material.
Photograph by Mark Aronica.

What, then, do architects quest for? Though their search may
contain some of the same goals of certainty, economy, and elegance
of the engineer, architectural goals would not normally be typified
by these values. The search of architecture has, in the past, revolved
around the particular rather than the general and the ability of the
particular to convey an idea of significance about the way in which
we occupy the world in our buildings. Thus instead of their being a
single truth in architecture, there are a series of buildings that can be
pointed at in particular that are proposed to convey ideas of architectural significance with unusual power and clarity. What is good
about a work of architecture is measured against the background of
the values of these significant structures. A value that exists in the
abstract but is never manifest in the form of a building quickly becomes a platitude that loses its compelling power among designers.
Architects look to their past not as much for models of form—though
they do so—as for validation of their current ideas. It is not that
new ideas cannot be developed through the thought of design but
that such values must be able to be reconciled with those that have
emerged from the great buildings of the past. This mode of thought
is the search for an understanding of the problem of inhabitation:

the discovery of why creating a place to dwell brings forth a previously inexplicit value inherent in the act of dwelling. The accretion of these awarenesses and the ideas to which they give rise forms the body of architectural knowledge.

The solar cube experiment spoke volumes about the measurable differences of solar apertures in collecting heat but was mute about the significance of this collection to the ideas of human habitation of space. The paintings of the second exercise suggested the significance of a room containing a table and chairs as a place to be in the sunlight but were mute about the quantifiable consequences of the windows.

And so method and desired knowledge turn out to be as different in engineering and architecture as were their respective views of space and use of symbols. The students who were asked to convert the thought of their physics experiments to the thought of design and to make the kinds of knowledge they were trying to arrive at using these two methods of thought synonymous were being asked to take on a Herculean task. For this reason, their failure seems so much more likely than success would have been. This problem is no less acute for the profession of architecture at large. In practice, the problem of the differences discussed in this chapter is never directly addressed. The two systems of thought are merely mashed together out of necessity through the agencies of political and economic power rather than by dealing with their conceptual differences.

Conceptual Differences between Engineering and Architecture as Technological Thought

It would appear from these distinctions that Reyner Banham's call for architecture to more seriously adopt engineering's technological ethic might be more difficult to achieve than it was initially thought to be. The rift between engineering and architectural definitions of technology in architectural thought runs deep.

The utilitarian efficiency that engineers seek from the use of technologies is, at its core, a different value from the architectural search for the way in which technologies create meaning for their inhabitants. These two visions of technology are not mutually exclusive, but neither are they synonymous. The distinctions of these two disciplines' visions of technology and design are consequential. They are not simple matters of semantics or of slightly different procedural proclivities, as some would contend. Their reconciliation is not simply a matter of finding a slightly more effective manner of translating information from one side of the rift to the other or of developing elevated skill in manipulating this information once transferred. They are not given to being reconciled in slogans, such as defining architecture as "the marriage of art and science," that reduce such distinctions to unhelpful platitudes. At the heart of this rift lies a conceptual division in human thought. This division constitutes a real dilemma for the discipline of architecture.

It would be naive to imagine that two such different intellectual enterprises could casually be reconciled simply because they share some portions of a common goal. Yet it would be just as naive to imagine that they could operate independently, each caring only for its particular concerns in using technology to make a building. The technologies of buildings are always required to meet the empirical tests that technologies have always had to undergo to demonstrate that they are, in actuality, an effective response to natural forces. Engineers possess far more potent constructs than do architects to ensure that building technologies meet this standard. Conversely, this empirical perspective poses a constant danger to architecture's need to deliver a figural symbolic view of the natural world that human beings inhabit. Without this proviso, the role of architecture in manipulating technology would collapse into that of engineering, reducing building technology solely to questions of utilitarian efficiency.

The problem for architecture in developing its own attitude toward technology returns us, albeit with greater insight, to the relationship of mechanics and meaning. There are many related ways to speak of this problem. It might be thought of as the relation of the utility of a tool to what that tool culturally comes to mean to a people. It might be thought of as the distinction between the measurable effectiveness of things that perform tasks well and the realm of art as ineffable ideas. It might be thought of as the difference between quantifiable values and those ideas that must be interpreted to have qualitative import. Or it might be thought of as the difference between the ideas that literal and figural symbols are able to enunciate. This list might be extended indefinitely, but at its heart, it would return to the same issue. If architectural technology is to exist both in a world of measurable empirical force and in a world of immeasurable ideas that give interpreted significance to the natural world, then a system of thought will need to be devised that is capable of housing all the foregoing differences.

3. Mending the Rift: Twentieth-Century Attempts to Reconcile Mechanics and Meaning

> Contemporary science has almost completely neglected the truly primordial problem that the phenomena of fire poses to the untutored mind.
>
> **Gaston Bachelard, *The Psychoanalysis of Fire***

Many twentieth-century commentators have attempted to understand the rift between an architectural and an engineering definition of technological thought as mechanics and as meaning. The four authors discussed in this chapter describe positions that are most familiar to architecture in this regard. Each commentator comes from a different background and thus defines the relationship of the mechanical utility of objects to their meaning as form from a different intellectual perspective. The importance of the positions that each puts forth is that they both by commission and by omission begin to outline the conditions necessary for developing an architectural stand on this issue.

Defining Positions

R. BUCKMINSTER FULLER AND THE COLLAPSE OF MEANING INTO MECHANICS

> Generalized design-science exploration is concerned with discovery and use by the human mind of complex aggregates of generalized principles in specific-longevity, special-case innovations designed to induce humanity's consciously competent participation in local evolution . . . [as the] cosmically unique functioning of humans in the generalized design scheme of the Universe.
>
> **R. B. Fuller, *Synergetics***

R. B. Fuller was an anomaly of twentieth-century specialization. He crossed the boundaries of science, engineering, architecture, philosophy, and evangelism with impunity. Fuller was admired by members of each of these fields but accepted by none as one of their own. His contribution to understanding the relationship of mechanics to meaning in architecture grows out of a deep belief that all there is to know about this issue may be found through insight into the structure of nature. If only human vision could pierce the veil of appearances to understand the underlying structure of natural phenomena, people could grasp the fundamental characteristics of what otherwise is a kind of blind, disorganized poking around in nature's apparatus. A firm understanding of the scientific structure of nature is thus the key to formulating technological solutions to human problems.

A good example of this kind of thought is Fuller's reference to the triangle rather than the rectangle, as the correct basis for formulating the gravity-resisting structure of a building. To Fuller, it was clear that nature had declared the triangle to be the form of structural choice. A triangle is inherently a stable form. Its shape cannot be changed without changing the length of its sides. A rectangle, conversely, is inherently an unstable form. The angles at the intersection of its sides can rotate without resistance. Therefore the rectangle is given to a kind of inherent desire to collapse that must be resisted by means other than the shape of its structure. To do so is a possible but abhorrent solution to the principles of the underlying form of the universe. The outcome of the application of this contention is manifest in the geodesic dome. The form of this structure is the logical outcome of the accretion of triangles. The proof of its goodness lies in the fact that it requires only one-sixth the material necessary to span a space of equal volume than would be required of a rectilinear structure. Economy of means, in this sense, is understood as a fundamental characteristic of natural structure to be discovered and emulated by human invention.

The outcome of this approach to architectural technology is apparent in the variety of geodesic domes that Buckminster Fuller designed but is more fundamentally located in the kind of design thought to which it gives rise. Under the agencies of this theory, technology is the sole province of nature. The definition of what it is, how it should work, and what its aims should be can be determined solely on the grounds of what nature is thought to be as a mechanical structure. Goodness of form is measured by the economy with which it is assumed that nature accomplishes its tasks. The goal of architectural technology is to attempt to approach the same

Fuller contended that nature preferred triangles as structural forms.
The outcome of this thought is manifest in this geodesic dome.
Photograph by Ma Weizhong.

economy of means. To do more with less includes all that there is to know about the way in which buildings resist gravity, modify climate, and transmit sunlight.

This approach to the problem of mechanics and meaning solves architecture's technological problem by collapsing meaning into mechanics. In technological logics such as that of the triangles of the geodesic dome, all interpretations that might arise from a non-empirical viewpoint are simply set aside as unimportant. Meaning and efficient operation are defined to be synonymous. Other values may exist, but they lie outside the domain of architectural technology.

HERBERT READ AND THE EVOLUTION OF MEANING FROM MECHANICS

> What I would like to establish, for all these early human artifacts, is an evolutionary sequence that passes through three stages: (1) conception of the object as a tool; (2) making and refinement of the tool to a point of maximum efficiency; (3) refinement of the tool beyond the point of maximum efficiency towards the conception of form-in-itself. . . . The problem is to determine at what point elegance ceases to be utilitarian, at what point form is divorced from function.
> **Herbert Read, "The Origin of Art as Form"**

In a second point of view, that of the noted art critic Herbert Read, the issue of the relationship of mechanics to meaning is seen in the evolution and implements of utility to become objects of purely symbolic value. As an art critic, Read is searching for the tie that led early people to decorate utensils as the precursor of art that served no utilitarian purpose. His theory thus centers on ways in which utensils such as the stone ax cease to have a functional purpose in their societies when they become ceremonial objects. Ceremonial objects, in this instance, are thought to be synonymous with pure artistic form.

Read documents this evolution in the transformation of axes, flasks, and hammers from useful utensils to symbols that are detached from their use. The way in which this transformation takes place, according to Read, is that a utensil is first discovered in its crudest form as it occurs in nature. People, for instance, discovered that certain shapes of rocks that they could hold in their hand would help them to cut wood more effectively than with their hands alone. This discovery then became part of tribal knowledge, to be transmitted from generation to generation until someone discovered that the effectiveness of this tool could be improved by chipping away at certain kinds of rocks with other rocks. This discovery of the human power to transform natural material to suit human purpose opened the door for continued refinement of tools. The edge of the stone could be made progressively sharper, and eventually a tree branch would be strapped to it to increase the leverage that could be brought to bear on a material that was to be cut. At some time, the ax as an instrument would come to be crafted in a manner that was better than it had to be. This crafting of the tool began to prefigure development beyond that of functional use. Fine craft as a means to make things that superseded a utilitarian conception of "good enough for use" was the precursor of the abstract values for which form might come to stand. This step over the functional boundary of thought about a tool was then able to give way to purely abstract notions of the object. The once useful ax could now be made of onyx that had little capacity to cut effectively but became instead the symbol of political power to be handed from tribal chief to tribal chief as the legitimization of the continuity of the right to that power.

For Read the central problem of symbolic form was that it served no instrumental purpose. Objects that continued to serve these purposes could easily be confused with vernacular crafts and hence not be regarded as legitimate objects of art. Thus to gain true artistic symbolic value, a utensil would have to give up all claim to serving a functional purpose. The evolution of instrumental form into symbolic form is, however, what is of interest in attempting to understand the relationship of meaning to mechanics in this viewpoint.

This teapot by Nicholas McDaniel shows how a utilitarian object that has been crafted beyond its functional requirements becomes a work of art.

Here, mechanics gives rise to the world of form as first discovered in nature. It selects some of these forms over others as having the potential to aid in the performance of tasks while diminishing the attention to natural objects that do not seem to display this potential. Once a form was selected, the reason to attempt to improve on the original form that nature lent to the enterprise was built into the reason for the selection in the first place. All that was required of human beings to modify this form to better suit their needs was the notion that such activity was possible. This was a discovery that might have taken a long time to occur but was essentially inevitable given the structure of the human mind and hand.

Once this seminal boundary of refinement of nature was crossed, the range of possibility for development was infinite. The next critical juncture in the development of meaning in this process was the ability to assign values to an object that has been refined for a purpose not literally in evidence in the use of that object. This is the great divide that allows form to represent an idea rather than to be an implement of action. For Herbert Read, this transformation must be complete for the object to assume the station of purely symbolic form, the form of the pure idea of art.

The way in which Read would attempt to solve architecture's technological problem would be to define the technology of the solar cube exercise to be a matter of utility and the sunlight of the painting to be capable of generating symbolic meaning. His artistic sympathies would understand the light of the painting as the search for the symbolic definition of place. The link between the solar cube and the light of the painting would look much like the link between the utilitarian ax refined beyond the needs of use and the ceremonial ax. Both emanate from the same technological form, but the ideas that the latter represents are not evidenced by the development of the former. Place is not a concept that emanates directly or organically from the performance of predicted conversions of visible light into heat. Rather, when this search for utility is transcended by the form of the sunlit room of the painting, it is able to communicate the pure symbolic idea of place. One would follow the other serially. The latter requires the development of the former but is not a predetermined outcome of it. The sunlight of the solar cube would have to cease to be useful to become the symbolically meaningful sunlight of the painting from this perspective.

AMOS RAPOPORT AND MECHANICS AS THE NONPARTICIPATORY
BOUNDARY OF MEANING

> The suggestion that social and cultural factors, rather than physical
> forces, are most influential in the creation of house form is an impor-
> tant reason for turning to primitive and vernacular building for a first
> look at house form. . . . The more forceful the physical constraints
> and the more limited the technology and command of means, the less
> are non-material aspects able to act. However, they never cease to
> operate.
>
> **Amos Rapoport, *House, Form, and Culture***

Amos Rapoport, in *House, Form, and Culture*, adds yet another argument to the nature of this relationship. From Rapoport's perspective as an anthropologist, science and engineering have made far too
much of the causal link between function, technology, and the resultant form of houses. His attack is correctly directed against deter-
minists who seek to prove that when people are left to their own devices, untrammeled by the tastes of overly self-conscious values,
they produce houses that emanate directly from the measurable conditions of their context, the level of technology that they have acquired to meet those conditions, and the resources that they have at
their disposal to do so. Rapoport points out that African tribes that
live in similar regions, possess similar levels of technological knowledge, and have access to similar resources construct homes of very
different forms. He ascribes the development of the form of these
houses, therefore, to social rather than technological needs. The relationship that he defines between the two is called "criticality." In
the terms of this relationship, technological requirements as mechanics bound the choice but do not determine the form of a house.
That determination is a function of a set of beliefs that include a
people's cosmological myths, the beliefs of their national and local
culture, and beliefs they might share with a small group of people or
hold as individuals. The greater the stress placed on a form by its
technological requirements, the more limited the range of choices
that are available to these social values; but this choice is never the
organic outcome of measurable physical need alone. Thus a rocket
ship that was being designed to go to the Moon would possess high
criticality and hence limited choice of form premised on social customs and beliefs. A house in Hawaii would suffer from few of these
constraints and hence be available to a wide range of choices of

form based on social customs and beliefs. Most buildings would represent low levels of criticality given this definition. The Eskimo igloo or the clean room of a modern laboratory building would represent exceptions, but in the main, buildings face few problems of exceptional levels of technological stress.

Here the relationship between mechanics and meaning is neatly partitioned into two worlds. One of the worlds bounds the other but does not directly participate in the creation of form. Form in architecture is thus characterized as that which carries social meaning that is developed within boundaries established by mechanics. Mechanics are denied a place in the actual act of this creation.

Rapoport would solve architecture's technological problem by allowing both the solar cube and the painting to have primacy, but in different ways. For Rapoport, the discovery that the visible light that came through a south-facing window could be effectively converted to heat would condition, but need not take any part in, the definition of a room as a place to be. In his contention there would be little problem in accepting that the painting of the light of the room containing a table and chairs would not emanate from this knowledge in any way. Such a division would, in fact, be consistent

The facade of this modest Minnesota house by Dale Mulfinger takes special care to convey values important to a suburban culture: the garage, the ceremonial front door, and the window of the master bedroom. Photograph by Dale Mulfinger.

with Rapoport's stance concerning the relationship between the two. Architects who used the painting instead of the solar cube exercise as the base of their designs would simply be establishing architectural form on the basis of cultural beliefs rather than allowing it to be determined as the outcome of empirical constraint.

SUSANNE LANGER AND THE COLLAPSE OF MECHANICS INTO MEANING

Art is the creation of forms symbolic of human feeling. The word "creation" is introduced here with full awareness of its problematical character. . . . An artifact as such is merely a combination of material parts, or a modification of a natural object to suit humam purposes. It is not a creation, but an arrangement of given factors. A work of art, on the other hand, is more than an "arrangement" of given things—even qualitative things. Something emerges from the arrangement of tones or colors which was not there before and this, rather than the arranged material, is the symbol of sentience."

Susanne Langer, *Feeling and Form*

Finally, there is the work of Susanne Langer concerning this issue. Langer too was waging war against the kind of determinism promoted by a belief in scientific method that has grown in Western culture since the seventeenth century. In *Philosophy in a New Key,* Langer asks if what philosophers term "rationality" can only be the outcome of scientific thought or whether rationality can also be the outcome of the arts. The question that she poses is "Is the music of Mozart irrational?" Certainly, this is a wonderfully provocative question to ask of the way in which contemporary society thinks of the arts in comparison with the way it regards scientific reasoning. The answer to this question lies for Langer in what the two modes of thought are attempting to accomplish and not in the efficacy of their methods as compared to an absolute value. Langer contends that just as science is a set of ideas that attempts to provide a structure for the occurrence of individual phenomena in the physical world, so the arts are a parallel framework for developing ideas that give a more general order to the feelings that individual human beings experience. She contends that there is no relationship between the two. A musical note may be physically measured to vibrate the air at a specific number of oscillations per minute, but the most profound knowledge of the physics of this phenomenon will never produce a musical composition of significant value. Put in different words, if Mozart had been vastly more knowledgeable than he was about the physics of the notes that he hurriedly scribbled on a score, the world would have been no better off. That is, Langer contends, because music and composition have nothing to do with physics. What they have to do with is the impact they have on the feelings of the people who hear this music and the ideas that emanate from those feelings. These listeners are moved by what has alternately been termed the "resonances and reverberations," the "dramatic import," the "realness," or, in Langer's terms, the "semblance of human feeling" that is initiated by the music. Music reaches into human beings in this construct where physics fears to tread. The metaphoric ideas of who we are, are conveyed by the arts. Human beings must look within themselves as a part of the corporate ideas that give significance to human feeling to understand how they, as a reflection of who they see themselves to be, belong to the world. As Langer justly points out, human feelings as the base of logic have been demeaned by a world that is committed to empiricism as the definition of fact, and fact as the definition of legitimate reasoning.

Langer would solve architecture's technological problem by contending that architects were looking in the wrong place when

A fragment of a musical score by Mozart illustrates
the kind of thought that interests Langer.

they looked to the mechanical performance of the solar cube to lend significance to human existence. That significance is unavailable to the thought of mechanics. Mechanics can describe the physics of a technological form accurately without stating anything about its human significance. What is significant to the operation of the natural world is thus relatively insignificant to the development of a human being's attempts to discover what it means to be human. The search for a place in the sunlight is a human pursuit in all terms of the word.

Langer thus conflates the world of mechanics and the world of meaning much as R. Buckminster Fuller did the opposite. In this viewpoint, meaning as a definition of the human condition is unavailable to the definition of the world as mechanics. The arts developed for just this reason. It is through the logic of the arts that meaning arises that allows human beings to understand why they perceive the world in the ways that they do. Mechanics can only discuss nature's conformance to empirical phenomena. It cannot develop an understanding of why those phenomena are meaningful to people.

Critique of These Positions

Each of these viewpoints is a well-reasoned, insightful, and well-crafted argument concerning the relationship of mechanics to meaning as this relationship pertains to the technology of architecture. Each has a good deal to offer in forging this definition, but none is complete and satisfactory within itself as an explanation of this relationship.

R. Buckminster Fuller correctly identifies that this relationship is initiated by the empirical characteristics of nature. Fuller is helpful in identifying that nature is an infinite source of information in the peculiarly human quest to understand things by understanding their underlying structure. The recurrent position of heavenly bodies in the sky might have been the source of the first human inkling that nature was not a random but rather a patterned set of events that manifest an underlying organization of the phenomena that surround human beings. Stonehenge was a celebration of that discovery in 2000 B.C.

The important point is not that any of these conceptions are correct but that we as human beings choose to see nature in these terms. Our perception of the structure of nature derives from an observation of it but always also reflects who we think we are. The need to envision nature as orderly is a human, not a natural, need.

Finally, Fuller's contention that we should look to the characteristics of that structure to better understand how to manipulate it not only is the ground of modern science but has always proven to be a highly effective technological strategy. It lends credence both to the modern-day positivists who can point to a seemingly endless array of new technologies that are the great-grandchildren of scientific understandings of the structure of nature and to the arguments of the ecologists who suggest that our technological tampering with nature is roughly akin to plunging a large screwdriver into the back of a finely crafted watch to fix it. There does appear to be an underlying structure to nature, and the human understanding of this structure is one of the constituent factors of human thought. In *The Ascent of Man,* Jacob Bronowski describes the acquisition of this kind of knowledge as "the hand as the cutting edge of the mind" (94–95). We take action on the natural environment, Bronowski contends, in ways that lay its structure bare. Hence the construction of a Gothic cathedral is a wonderful metaphor for the pursuit of modern science. In the cathedral, rock has been split from its mindless quarry revealing the mindful pattern in the stone as it is majestically reassembled in the great flying buttresses and soaring vaults of Chartres or Notre Dame or Amiens.

But as essential and profound as this kind of knowledge is to the pursuits of human beings, it is not adequate to the task of explaining the full relationship of mechanics to meaning in the buildings that we construct. For that to be the case, human beings would be required to limit their definitions of their own significance within the underlying structure of nature to those ideas that emanate from an empirical knowledge of nature. People would

Eight hundred years after their conception, the flying buttresses of a Gothic cathedral remain compelling testimony to both the power and the richness of natural force as an initiator of architectural form.

be forced to describe their own character in the same terms as they described the character of their natural context. That would leave them with the interesting dilemma of proposing that the natural world was animated by spirit that they possess in the form of human consciousness, or with doing away with their definition of themselves as having this quality. The human feelings and thoughts that do not have physical analogues would have to be eliminated to fit people's new empirical model of themselves. Although this may be the long-term hope of positivists, it is not consistent with the way in which we choose to describe ourselves today. People are, to themselves, a rich and complex interweaving of intellect, emotion, and sometimes spirit. They are human precisely because they defy the boundaries of the inanimate world in their own minds.

Evidence of the insufficiency of Fuller's contention that meaning is contained in mechanics is found in the paucity of meaning that may be ascribed to his geodesic domes as architectural constructions. These domes attempt to be analogous to underlying natural structure, and they demonstrate their effectiveness in reaching this goal in their efficiency. Their objective, as is the goal of all engineered works, is to eliminate all superfluous material as the limits of the performance of that material are probed. Geodesic domes may or may not reach this goal, but their instinct to do so is clear. The outcome is a definition of the underlying structure of nature as an admiration of efficient structural shapes. This would not seem to be a particularly satisfying definition of our natural context either in human terms or in the way in which this relationship is manifest in architecture. There is in Fuller's efficient structures, moreover, the clear and abiding sense that there is a great deal more to this relationship than can be conveyed by the search for meaning in the limits of performance of materials. There is a strange emptiness to Fuller's work that requires that it be populated by other forms not only to become useful but, more fundamentally, to broaden its base of interpretation as being of human, as well as of technological, significance. This gap is the gap of meaning that demonstrates that human perceptions of the significance of their place in nature are not contained wholly in the mechanics that define the way in which the natural world appears empirically to operate.

Herbert Read's position in this regard is interesting because his quest is to connect the very ideas that Fuller would disconnect. Read offers productive insight into the question of mechanics and meaning primarily because he begins this search in the discovery and making of everyday tools. This is the very ground of technology. The addition of the methods of modern science to these constructions is simply the latest in a series of ways of conceiving of our tools. In spite of the insight granted by science, technology remains, for the most part, the province of hands-on inventors. Architectural technology remains, to a great degree, the offspring of empirical toolmaking. It is in the process of making a tool, and not in abstract definitions of it as numerical force, that much insight is gained into the character of what it could or should be. Moreover, making a tool requires direct contact with the material from which it is made. The possibilities of the utility of the tool are inherent in the characteristics of this material, but so are all its other characteristics. The tool is not a reduction of material to a definition of effective response to natural force but rather an accretion of all the other qualities that individual materials may possess in addition to the potential for usefulness. Work-

Fuller's geodesic domes emanate from an understanding of gravity that has much in common with the kind of thought that propelled the creation of the Gothic flying buttress, but unlike the buttresses, a strange sense of emptiness accompanies these mechanical domes. Photograph by John Carmody.

ing the material to create tools of progressively greater efficiency cannot help but bring attendant characteristics of the material and the forms that it might create forward in the mind of the toolmaker. His or her knowledge of the structure of the natural world as empirical force is thus mediated because he or she comes to understand that structure not in itself but in the shaping of material to reveal it.

Read's definition of the apparent will of human beings to move beyond the effective boundaries of efficiency in making tools poses a problem for dedicated mechanists. If understanding underlying structure through finding the limits of performance of materials under nature's stress is the purpose of architectural technology, what conceivably could be the rationale for seeking solutions to problems that are more efficient than they need to be? Is there really an innate human urge that, according again to Jacob Bronowski,

The urge to develop tools beyond the point of maximum efficiency permeates architectural technology, as in this detail from the structure of the Centre Georges Pompidou.

suggests that "having done it well, he loves to do it better" (116)? This contention leads to a conclusion that the reason for creating the tool as a useful way of manipulating the forces of nature is now being challenged by the maker's sense of the power of his or her own ability to craft material. The tool is no longer simply a utensil but rather a manifestation of the skill of its maker. It has become a rather strange mixture of identification of natural force and definition of human attributes. The significance of this shift from response to empirical need to a fondness for craft in and of itself is that an elevated level of craft is unnecessary to the performance of the task at hand. If Read's contention that toolmaking is crafted beyond the point of usefulness is accepted, then the spectrum of all that might be represented through the process of this craft opens up.

Read's contention that the tool must cease to perform utilitarian purpose in order to become an object that might be regarded as containing symbolic content represents a problem if architectural technology is to become anything more than a well-crafted tool. Frames of buildings must go on resisting gravity if a building is to stand. Envelopes must go on resisting the flow of heat through them if comfortable climatic conditions are to be maintained within a building. Windows must go on transmitting light to the interior of a building if it is to be illuminated with sunlight. All architectural technologies are required, in fact, to go on performing utilitarian tasks no matter what other claims are made for them. This responsibility is the essence of what makes them technological. It is the chief ingredient that differentiates technological from all other architectural forms. To do away with its utilitarian prowess would be to do away with the very essence of architectural technology. To maintain this function, however, under Read's definition would be to deny the possibility that these elements of architecture could convey symbolic meaning.

Perhaps a solution to this dilemma might be arrived at by re-examining Read's premise. For Read, an object of art becomes such precisely because it serves no utilitarian purpose. Being relieved of utilitarian function allows art to deal with what might be termed a higher realm of thought: that which symbolically rather than literally places human beings in their existence. This is the realm of ideas rather than the realm of acts, and so the two must be cleaved apart with exactitude. To confuse the two would be to confuse the primary differentiation between two distinctly different modes of human thought. But to cleave these two modes of thought so cleanly apart seems to be an arbitrary choice in this case. It would seem to be just as logical to assume that the symbolic characteristics of an ax, for instance, were inherent in its first discovery as a tool. Is there such a great leap between the knowledge in action that an ax extends human physical powers to the confirmation of political power through the passing on of a ceremonial ax? Is human thought so tightly compartmentalized that thinking in one area of life does not give rise to conceptions in another? Why should the boundaries of metaphorical reasoning be unable to transcend the gulf between

The problem with Read's contention is evident in the construction of this wall in Katsura Imperial Palace in Kyoto, Japan, which continues to perform the utilitarian task of separation yet becomes an object of art.

practical action on the world to become a set of ideas about the significance of being in the world?

The latter would seem to be a far more likely way of conceiving of the relationship of mechanics to meaning than Read's more narrow position. To rob the ceremonial ax of its origin in extending human prowess in the physical world would be to eliminate the essential origin of the idea. The meaning of political power is certainly different as a symbol of authority than is the ax as a utensil of practical use, but the two concepts inhabit the same form because they share the same conceptual roots. The possibility, perhaps even the necessity, of extending the function of a tool to become symbolic meaning is inherent in all purposeful reshaping of natural material. It is not an arbitrary relation that is forged through these mechanical acts of technology but a constrained initiation of conceptual thought in effective action.

Amos Rapoport's discussion of the relationship of mechanics and meaning in *House, Form, and Culture* presents a slightly different set of possibilities and problems in ascertaining the definition of this relationship in architectural technology. Rapoport's contention that meaning is a culturally versus mechanically housed concept seems to have great merit. If culture is, in fact, the sum of a society's

In passive solar houses, the architecturally fecund proposition that a house has a front that addresses a larger cultural realm is reduced to the mechanics of a transparent surface that gathers the sun's rays. This transparent surface is roughly akin to moving the furnace from the basement of the house to become its facade.

agreed-upon values, then it would be difficult to imagine the development of human meaning outside those boundaries. His second assertion, that those values are manifest in the form of buildings, a form that is not simply the direct translation of scientific fact into the organization of the material of a structure, again appears to be borne out in the differences in the forms of the houses that his book examines. The critical addition that Rapoport makes to the present discussion is that meaning in architecture is constituted of the values that a population comes to believe are manifest by a particular design, and that those values are presented to people as form. To the more scientifically inclined who consider architectural technology as engineering, form is only a necessary evil required to transmit

Rapoport's concern with socially derived cultural meaning seems to
be developed at the expense of human experience. This corner of a
thatched-roof house connotes a rich range of cultural thought that is
developed from technological purpose.

or retard the transmission of quantities of natural force. Meaning is
housed completely in their ability to do so, making the range of
other human values superfluous. The outcome of this kind of position is found in the passive solar homes that convert the south elevation to a furnace and the organization of the interior into the order
of ductwork. Rapoport's suggestion that these solutions to the problem of the house have lost meaning in an attempt to dictate their
form as the direct and scientifically logical outcome of their measurable operation seems to be confirmed by the uneasiness that such
technically dominated solutions to buildings produce. While one
may admire the ingenuity or efficiency of these buildings, it would be
quite another matter to inhabit the level of architectural meaning (or
lack of the same) that these buildings exhibit. Technological determinism is not a fruitful road to rich cultural meaning.

In Rapoport's discussion, architectural form is able to deliver its
meaning because of its relationship to social structures. The political
organization of the tribe, its cosmological myths, the organization of
the family, and the role of women are major factors in the final determination of the form of the house. This is borne out in the specificity of architectural organizations of these houses at scales that

range from the camp as a whole to the places that family members take at the table to eat. Although Rapoport presents an interesting case for the architectural forms that he does discuss, there is an equally interesting lack of discussion of forms that might not fit this model quite as well. Where, for instance, does he discuss the fact that all these dwellings have floors and that the floors do something as well as mean something? What about the walls and roofs of these dwellings? Do the cultural meanings of the wall as separation from inhospitable climatic conditions and the roof as covering from the sky depend only on the social order of the tribe or family? Where is the place for meaning to emerge through the making of the house as an implement that was so powerful in Herbert Read's vision of the relationship between mechanics and meaning? To substitute a kind of social determinism for technical determinism would appear only to restate the long-standing philosophical distinction between nature and culture without doing much to reveal how they might relate to each other.

If the house is a function of cultural meaning as Rapoport asserts, the question remains where those cultural meanings arise from. In his desire to eradicate the kind of technological determinism that would demean cultural meaning as a powerful determiner of form, Rapoport forges an impenetrable distinction between utilitarian function that arises from human needs and cultural values that arise from social beliefs. It would seem improbable that a people's efforts to construct a house in the context of the natural forces of gravity, sunlight, and climate would not leave a mark on their consciousness that would be carried into their mythologies concerning the essence of the natural world they inhabit. The possibility of taking technological action in the world without forging at least the initiation of cultural thought about the value of that world seems equally unlikely.

Susanne Langer offers what might be considered to be the argument that is most distant among these four from the question of meaning and mechanics in architectural technology, but any argument concerning the characteristics of this relationship would be incomplete if it did not address the general viewpoint and problem that Langer puts forth. If Langer is correct in her assertions, mechanics are as void of understandable meaning as are the vibrations of a musical note when not intentionally combined with other notes. Middle C certainly means something, but it does not mean a late

Beethoven string quartet. Langer's interesting argument is that the meaning of what might otherwise be considered merely a string of dissociated notes not only is housed in Rapoport's definition of culture but penetrates the human psyche more deeply than the more empirical construct of culture might suggest. Her contention that art gives form to the idea of human feelings allows this construct to cross the boundaries of time, place, and culture. Whereas some human feelings may be the product of a specific culture, a broad range of feelings have occurred to all peoples over all their history. There is thus a seminal core to human feeling. It is a core that allows contemporary people to empathize with the problems of long-dead generations of forebears, and for peoples of different nationalities and beliefs to recognize their common humanity. It is the reason why dance is as cathartic for people today as it was when first devised thousands of years ago. It is the reason why great music is so moving to generations of people who are no longer aware of the social and political conditions that gave rise to it.

The condition that Langer places on the meaningful transmission of human feelings in art is that the idea of those feelings, not the feelings themselves, is being transmitted. This is a critical construct in this theory because the role of the word "idea" here is to gather what otherwise might remain personal though deeply moving thought into a form that might be recognized as having meaning for a large number of people. The "idea" of feelings explores the underlying structure of the emotions felt by each of us as individuals just as science explores the underlying structure of what would otherwise remain a series of dissociated physical phenomena. The process of conducting this search creates a framework in which other phenomena might be located. This framework both organizes individual data into larger categories and, in the logic of the assembly, reveals the underlying significance of the phenomena to human thought. Langer's schema thus attempts to categorize the facts of art in terms of the way they address human feelings and in so doing reveals how these feelings give birth to a form of human reasoning.

What this contention brings to the discussion of architectural technology is the possibility of meaning that includes not only empirical fact but also the ideas of human feeling. We experience the world around us with all our senses and with all our human abilities to think. These are not neatly partitioned off into those forms of human thought that apply to natural conditions and those that are

"The Sun Worshiper,"
by Nicola Moss. The
sculpture is symbolic
of our sense that the
sun propels all life.

reserved for human intercourse. The world comes to the minds of human beings as a piece. The divisions of thought that have been placed on the perception of technology that gives primacy to the abstractions of mathematical thought are productive but nonetheless artificial limitations on the way in which mechanics might come to have meaning for human beings.

The central issue here is not whether Susanne Langer is correct in her formulation of this issue but that she is attempting to explain what many others have tried to explain. This is the commonly held understanding that human existence seeks significance in modes of thought other than those of science, and that these other modes of thought are not secondary but are other primary human means of coming to terms with the problem of understanding our human existence.

Such a contention makes technology in architecture as a mediator between human beings and nature available to wide range of human thought. It no longer need be contained in the algorithms of mathematics. Its ability to comment on experiences that are significant to human existence permeates our deepest feelings as abstractions as well as those ideas that might emanate from thinking in words or in numbers. Meaning in architectural technology thus becomes available to the whole of a human being's body and mind.

The problem with this contention in terms of understanding mechanics and meaning is that in its desire to make human feeling of parallel value to science as a way of thinking about the world, it collapses the possibility of interpreted meaning, ideas that are a function of formal rather than literal symbols, into the world of art. Formal symbols become unavailable to mechanics, in Langer's theory, because mechanics are defined as a function of literal symbols alone. The number of vibrations that create a musical note is that number per second and none other. Therefore there are two worlds of thought forged in this contention, with no real way of communicating between them. Science and its derivative ways of explaining the phenomena of the world are able to bring meaning to human existence only inasmuch as they are able to accurately describe physical phenomena so that they might be equally as accurately predicted or controlled. Art, conversely, organizes the ideas of human feelings, from which their significance might be known. There are no correspondences between the two. The physical world of nature would therefore not appear to be able to bear metaphorical meaning in human thought as anything other than art. Technology, which is initiated in the literal possibility of transforming the world of nature, is effectively barred from participating in the realm of the ideas of human emotions in the completeness of this bifurcation of the world of human thought.

Conditions for Reconciling Mechanics and Meaning

The thoughts and conditions that emerge from this discussion point the way toward an architectural reconciliation of mechanics and meaning in the use of technology.

As this dock extends into the mist of the lake, it conjures dual images of the tangibility of the constructed object and the mystery of the world in which we place such objects.

This definition should admit to architectural technology's origin in an empirical understanding of natural force without succumbing to a definition of quantifiable utility as the all-pervasive value of technology in architecture. It should help architects to understand how acts that originate in a search for utility come to have symbolic meaning that extends beyond the boundaries of efficiency without abandoning the conceptual potential for thought that was embedded in its inception as a thing of use. It should treat technology as a cultural fact as opposed to maintaining the gulf between nature and culture that this kind of technology inherently crosses. And finally, it should connect the mechanics of technology to the ideas of human feeling as a reflection of the full breadth of ways that the world of nature becomes meaningful to its inhabitants.

But in the final analysis, an amalgam of the characteristics of these four positions will not produce a completely satisfying resolution to the issue of the relationship of mechanics to meaning in architectural technology. Although each position contributes valuable insights into the character that such a definition must assume, none attacks the heart of the problem. Such a resolution can be developed only by examining the roots of this dichotomy—the way in which we choose to define natural force itself.

4. The Map and the Territory

> The description we write will inevitably be a composite, a reworking
> of a hundred-odd descriptions that have dissolved together inside.
> For I don't think that we ever really forget what we read any more
> than we forget what we experience.
>
> **Sven Birkerts, *The Gutenberg Elegies***

Rethinking the Definition of Natural Forces

Have we as a people forgotten how to inhabit nature? Has this knowledge succumbed, as in Birkerts's fear for the private intellectual space of reading, to the virtual world of technologies that distance us from the meaning of palpable experience? Is it any more possible to forget our experience of the natural world than it is to forget what we have read, as Birkerts suggests? Do our descriptions of nature "dissolve together inside," as he contends that they do, to become a composite that unconsciously emerges in all our acts and thoughts?

These are strange questions to ask of a domain of thought that is normally characterized by the more certain terms of measurement and calculation. But they are the right questions to ask of architectural technology because they ask not what it has to do with nature but what it has to do with us. This is the question that gathers together concerns for the technological forms of my winter-morning window, the difference between the solar cube exercise and the painting of sunlight, and the descriptions of technology that emerge from the writings of Fuller, Read, Rapoport, and Langer. It asks why and how we should take note of our natural context through the forms that we make as habitational technologies.

The four propositions of the last chapter accomplished a great deal in framing an answer to this question, but they did so in a way that helped to give substance to the edges of this problem but left the center vacant. These authors divide creative acts into two fundamental categories: origins and outcomes. Fuller and Read specify the origin of creative acts to be external and empirical; Rapoport

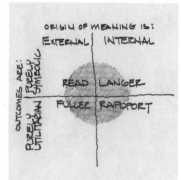

This diagram portrays the positions of Fuller, Read, Rapoport, and Langer concerning the origins and outcomes of creative acts.

and Langer specify that their source is a quality that stems from internal characteristics of human beings. The outcomes of these acts are similarly divided into categories of the useful and the purely symbolic. Read pairs external origins to symbolic outcomes, Fuller pairs external origins with utilitarian outcomes, Langer pairs internal origins with symbolic outcomes, and Rapoport pairs internal origins with utilitarian outcomes. Each proposed characteristics of this problem—its origin in an empirical nature, its promotion of common utensils to symbolic status, the understanding of architectural form as cultural significance, the recognition of the importance of human feeling to the generation of thought—but none was able to capture and give a place to any of the others within their explanation of the relationship of mechanics to meaning. What kind of thought might be placed in this center to hold these edges together?

The answer to this question may lie in the epigraph by Gaston Bachelard that began the last chapter: "Contemporary science has almost completely neglected the truly primordial problem that the phenomenon of fire poses to the untutored mind." In this quotation, Bachelard compresses the whole of the problem that confronts architectural technology as mechanics and meaning into a single sentence. If science has ignored what fire means to us as a lived phenomenon, then the calculations of engineering must surely be mute testimony to the truly primordial problem of building technologies. The notion of the "untutored mind" notes that normal human experience does not take stock of nature as scientific abstractions. Science defines fire by well-understood chemical transactions that characterize oxidation. However, it is not a series of abstract chemical reactions that any of us observe or cherish when we sit in front of a hearth on a cold winter night. The fire in that fireplace and the warmth that we feel from it are filled with all the associations that come from our own individual experience of fire and those of all the peoples who have preceded us in their experience of this fire. All have left a mark on our consciousness about what fire has come to mean. The contemporary fire might be explained as the scientific abstraction of oxidation, but it also retains the rich possibility of all primordial empirical experiences of being relived and reunderstood as a human event.

We have not forgotten how to live in nature. Our memory of how to do so has simply been dulled by thermostats, electric light switches, and hot water heaters. All these latter-day machines make our lives more convenient, easy, and comfortable. None of us really appreciates a cold shower. But beneath our appreciation for these machines lies another part of our sense of ourselves. This substructure of our minds searches for meaning in our experience of nature whether it is mediated by machines or not. It doesn't dismiss these machines, but it does ask of them if the human experience that they give birth to is "real" in the sense in which Michael Benedikt uses this word in his book *For an Architecture of Reality.* There are no easy answers to this question. A Dvořák quartet on the CD player may be just as meaningful to us as a live performance of the same. But our mind does differentiate between the two. We are able to discriminate between those of our experiences that touch us at deep levels and those of our experiences, no matter how convenient, comfortable, and pleasant, that don't.

In Bachelard's contention, this search for significance returns human thought to the fire in a way that science is unable to contemplate. Fire is an empirical phenomenon of the natural world, but unlike oxidation as a chemical process, it cannot adequately be defined as a mechanical process. It is not an abstraction but contains the fullness of reality as a lived human experience. But as a phenomenon of nature, it is also unlike other human experiences that are not anchored in the kind of empiricism to which nature gives birth. There is a difference between the human understanding of love as a condition of affection and fire as warmth, though the latter may be used metaphorically to describe the former. There is, then, a unique niche in the human mind that is set aside to search for the significance of nature as a tangible context for our lives. Oxidation is one map of this phenomenal terrain, but it is neither the only map nor the one most representative of the richness of the actual terrain in our corporate and individual experience of nature's territory.

The map that Bachelard creates to help to explain the "untutored mind's" appreciation for the phenomenon of fire suggests the possibility that the frames, weather envelopes, and windows that characterize primary architectural technology might be understood in the same way. The promise of such a map is that it might contain much that science and engineering are unable to represent about natural territory. Perhaps such a map can help us to remember how we live in nature.

The first condition for making a Bachelardian map of architectural technology is to define the terrain that the map is attempting to represent. The origin of human understanding of the natural world is located in the human ability to feel natural forces. Quantification is, in this sense, no more than a means to give the human experience of felt force a precise value. Though such precision lies outside normal human sensual capacities, it stems from them. The tangible but imprecise human experience of natural force as heavy, cold, and bright is extended and made precise through abstraction as the foot pounds of force on a beam, the literal difference between indoor and outdoor temperatures, and the foot-candles of light on a surface located 30 inches above the floor. But the core of this precision remains with the human capacity to feel the difference between 5 and 10 pounds, between 50 and 60 degrees Fahrenheit, and between 5 and 15 foot-candles of light.

This sensual ability to notice differences in the amount of natural force is, however, only a part of a broader framework of human discrimination. These differences are noticed by people in all the terms that might stem from being felt. Hence while gravity is felt as weight, it is also perpetual; while climate is temperature, it is also spring as rebirth; and while sunlight is foot-candles, it is also the horizon as the extent of a human domain. Here lies the linchpin of understanding natural force in other than purely mechanical terms: *Each human sense of natural force carries with it a far broader range of ideas than might be expressed in literal symbols because these forces are, and always have been, integral parts of human lives and thought.* Like all other commodities that make up the sum of this existence, the qualities of natural force have been probed, defined, and incorporated in the human mind to become a strand in the complex fabric of our existence. There are no simple mechanisms in that being, just as fire is not adequately explained in our everyday experience as oxidation.

Nature as Felt Force
If natural forces are identified as the product of literal symbols alone, then the only answer to the question of how mechanics relate

to meaning in buildings must be stated as quantity. The importance of reframing natural force in nonnumeric terms of felt force as their origin is that this redefinition returns these forces to a universe of human experience capable of metaphoric interpretation and hence of being the ground of symbolic speculation. Nature defined in its more primitive sense as felt force gives rise to Fuller's call for the empirical base of architectural technology, but it also accommodates Read's demand for a notion of symbolic meaning to arise from utilitarianism, Rapoport's claim that the meaning of architectural form is housed in culture, and Langer's contention that human feelings tell us much about our place in the world that science is unable to comprehend. In this more primitive vision of the natural world, action, symbol, corporate meaning, and human feeling have yet to be disassembled by the specialization of thought. The failure of the solar cube exercise gave fair warning that mechanics as literal symbols do not create ideas that readily participate in the manipulation of architectural technology as a formal symbol. Numerical calculations might follow creation in this view of architectural technology as a postgenerative measure of efficiency, but they cannot influence the initiation of formal thought. In the intellectual bifurcation of nature that forms the basis of Fuller's, Read's, Rapoport's, and Langer's examinations of the relationship of mechanics to meaning lies the reason for their inability to be reconciled by these proposals. Nature as felt force rather than as numeric amount might give them the ground necessary to do so. Looking to the human perception of these forces before they became objectified and quantified is akin to Bachelard's search for the meaning of fire before science foreclosed the possibility of this search.

The reconciliation of mechanics and meaning as felt force that gives rise to architectural technology does not always take place in an explicit manner in this mind because the idea is lodged so deeply in the human psyche. As a species, we have always inhabited the world as natural force that was felt. Gravity, climate, and sunlight have always been intimate partners in our occupation of the world. This intimacy has always directly conditioned the human experience. The marks left by this intimate relationship on the human mind and its thought are thus as old as the species itself.

Technology in architecture is a special case of understanding nature as felt force because notions of architectural technology have always literally and symbolically developed from this experience.

Technological form in architecture simply restates what has been learned by people about the means to provide shelter in a hostile world that was initiated by the first actions that were designed to transform that world to meet human needs. What was learned from these tangible acts has been redefined to meet the requirements of numerical or verbal symbols in human thought, but the core of this meaning remains locked in the forms that generated these secondary symbolic descriptions of their operation and purpose.

Constructing Maps of Natural Force

There are, then, not one but three possible maps that might represent the territory of architectural technology. The first grows from modern science's conception of nature as mathematical objectification. These principles are brought to bear on utilitarian problems by the second map of engineering. The third, as in Bachelard's contention that there is a fire of the scientifically untutored mind that represents the complexity and richness of the lived experience of nature, grows from the human capacity to viscerally feel natural force as the basis for developing associations with that force. This is the map of nature as felt force.

GRAVITY MAPPED BY SCIENCE

Gravity is defined by Newtonian science as an attraction of masses that is directly proportional to their magnitude and inversely proportional to the square of their distance from each other. The cause of this attraction is unknown. Newton described it as "certain forces by which the particles of bodies, by some cause hitherto unknown, are either mutually impelled towards one another . . . or are repelled and recede from one another." Scientific thought concerning the origin of gravity has advanced little over the succeeding three hundred years. It remains the single force of nature that cannot be integrated into a unified force theory in quantum mechanics. Thus gravity is known to science as its effects rather than as its cause. The Newtonian definitions of these effects serve well to describe the problem of resisting gravity inherent in the creation of buildings.

GRAVITY MAPPED BY ENGINEERING

This attraction of the mass of the earth for all objects that attempt to be separated from its surface is defined by engineering as loads. There are two basic categories of weight as the measure of this attraction with which buildings are conventionally defined as coping. The first are called dead loads because they are the weight of the material that is designed to resist the pull of the earth's mass and thus must remain stationary. The second are a transient set of weights comprising temporary masses such as snow on the roof or equipment, furniture, and people on the floor of a building. These are called live loads, as they are both the served weights of a structure and are capable of changing over time. These two kinds of attractions are resisted by what are termed the structural characteristics of different building materials as they are asked to assume different responsibilities in separating mass from the surface of the earth. The first responsibility is that of the column, which is asked to bring both the live and dead loads of a structure vertically to the earth. This material is said to be given to failure under these loads either by being crushed by them or by buckling. The second element of structure is asked to complete the possibility of enclosure that has been initiated by the column as it spans between columns to cover space from the sky. These elements are called beams and are given to failure by bending or by shear as they gather and concentrate the dispersed loads that occur along their length as they bring these loads to columns. When a load might be resisted directly by placing a structural member between it and the pull of the earth, the measure of the magnitude of the pull of gravity is in units of stress. When this pull is resisted indirectly so that resistant material tends to rotate about a point, it is called a moment. The capacity of a specific material to resist gravity is thus found in its ability not to be crushed, in its compressive or tensile capacity to resist being bent, or in its internal resistance to material sliding past other material under stress and thus failing in shear. Any particular arrangement of columns and beams can create a wide range of variations on these basic themes, but the core of this engineering system is the ability to assign numerical magnitude to the ways in which structural elements are most likely to fail.

GRAVITY MAPPED AS FELT FORCE

Gravity as felt force has always been sensed by people in the heaviness of objects. Before people measured the force of gravity in pounds, the ability of the earth to attract all things to its surface ordered the way people perceived objects. It gave the order of that which was closest to, and farthest away from, the earth as up and down, as top and bottom. Its regularity over space bequeathed a

The architectural map of gravity contains both of these former maps but converts their information to that which might be gleaned from tangible objects.

regular pattern on architectural elements that held other elements aloft. It gave relative size to elements being held overhead as they gathered progressively larger portions of gravity in hollowing out a space for human habitation within this force. These elements could not be moved or removed without causing the dissolution of this void and thus initiated a conception of permanence that is associated with the frame in architecture. Unlike any other human experience, gravity does not change over space or time. Gravity is the most orderly and consistent of all human experiences and hence gives birth to mental conceptions of regularity and permanence.

SUNLIGHT AS MAPPED BY SCIENCE

Sunlight is the product of the thermonuclear reaction that takes place in the core of the sun. Part of the energy released by this transformation of mass into energy is a bandwidth of radiation to which the human eye is sensitive. This specific range of frequency of electromagnetic radiation creates the spectrum of visible light and its hues of colors from blue to red. Again, what science determines to be light depends on effects that it creates rather than on understanding its structure. There are well conceived and carefully carried out experiments that demonstrate clearly that light is made up of particles that have mass, and there are just as convincing experiments that demonstrate that light consists of massless waves. The Newtonian definition of natural light serves architecture well. Newton demonstrated that sunlight was made up of radiation of various wavelengths that could be separated into primary colors when refracted through a glass prism. White is the combination of all these wavelengths.

SUNLIGHT AS MAPPED BY ENGINEERS

Lighting engineers have quantified the performance of light as the level of visible energy that emanates from a source versus that which is reflected by a surface at some distance from that source.

The Neolithic burial marker in southwest England conveys the sense that
gravity attaches us to the earth in a primitive and nakedly powerful way.

The measure of light at its source is in lumens; the measure of the reflection of light at its destination is in foot-candles.

The engineering problem of light in buildings is one of origins and distribution. The artificial origin of the light of a building is normally a luminaire. This is an electric lighting fixture that consists of the means to convert electricity to visible wavelength radiation and the means to direct that radiation at its target. There are a range of bulb types employed in the former and an equally broad range of reflectors and baffles to accomplish the second. If the form in which electricity comes to the luminaire in is inappropriate to the bulb type, then a ballast may also be necessary to convert alternating to direct current at appropriate voltages. Each of these components affects the efficiency of the luminaire as it converts electricity to light. Lighting engineers are, however, normally more concerned with the distribution and levels of light that are reflected by surfaces than they are with the efficiency of the luminaire. The goal of their work is too ensure that all areas of a building are lit to a level that allows all necessary tasks that depend on specified light levels to be performed easily. This is a difficult problem to solve under conditions of variable use and the differences in visual needs of different people. The outcome of this uncertainty has been the establishment of different lighting standards for different uses of space. Sunlight may be considered by these engineers as a light source, but its dependability and the difficulty inherent in controlling a dynamic light source make it suspect among many lighting engineers.

SUNLIGHT MAPPED AS FELT FORCE

Sunlight as felt force has always been sensed by people in their ability to see all that surrounds them. Before there was the measurement of light as foot-candles there was the rising and setting of the sun. As surfaces reflect sunlight each in their own particular way, the domain of form is created. As a reflection of the sun's light, this domain has a birth and death, a near and far, a soft and hard, a distinct and vague. The position of the sun in the sky locates human beings in time and space on the earth. Its rhythmic movement is mirrored in the birth and death of plants and animals and finally in the way in which human longevity is measured. The sun bounds and animates the formal domain of people as it connects the immutable heavens intimately to the mutable earth. Its light places all things in a relative position. We are here because we can see that we are not there.

An architectural definition of sunlight is less interested in absolute or
relative amounts of illumination than in the architectural ideas that the
formal manipulation of natural illumination is able to create,
as in Tadao Ando's Church of Light.

We are now because in a moment the sun will move in the sky and it
will be then.

CLIMATE AS MAPPED BY SCIENCE

Of the three natural forces that provide the foundation of this
study, only the last one, climate, is derivative. It is a natural force in
which sunlight and the surface of the earth interact to create a giant
and infinitely complex heat-driven machine. As different surfaces of
the earth become more or less normal to the sun's rays, they become
more efficient at absorbing and reradiating these rays as heat. This
process is affected not only by cloud cover but by the material that
makes up the earth's surface. Portions of the surface covered with
bare earth, sand, water, snow, and vegetation absorb and reradiate
sunlight as heat at different rates. This reradiated sunlight heats the
atmosphere and oceans unevenly, compelling the air and water to
attempt to equalize resultant pressure differences, yielding winds
and ocean currents. Solar energy also heats the surface of bodies of
water in a way that encourages a portion of the water to turn to
vapor and be absorbed into the body of the air. This vapor will

The dome at the Alhambra makes tangible and metaphoric reference
to a cosmos that envelops us from above as it gives temporal order to
the events of our lives and domains.

eventually become clouds as it rises and cools. Finally, it will return to the surface of the earth in a variety of forms of moisture that are dictated by the thermal conditions that house this process.

The energies that initiate climate and its interactions can be specified with great certainty. What cannot be determined with any great degree of confidence are the effects of the system. The process is made complex because the sun heats every portion of the earth differently, creating an ever changing set of energies attempting to reach a state of equilibrium in this great machine. As every energy moves to create its own local equilibrium, an entirely new set of conditions is produced globally that must attempt to reach the equilibrium of the whole, and thus the entire network of climatic energies is in a perpetual state of flux. They will never achieve their goal, but they will always attempt to do so.

CLIMATE AS MAPPED BY ENGINEERING

Engineers measure climate in three ways. The first of these has to do with the relationship of ambient climatic conditions with climatic standards under which most people would be comfortable performing specified tasks. A graphic formulation of this relationship is called the bioclimatic chart. This chart generally compares the range of relative humidity and air temperatures of different months of the year of a specific locale with a narrow band of temperature and associated relative humidity conditions (70 to 80 degrees Fahrenheit at 20 to 80 percent relative humidity) that most people would be comfortable at when normally dressed. The purpose of this chart is to understand the kind and size of climatic stress that occurs in any locale at specific times of the year.

The second of these measures is one that seeks to understand the rate at which climatic conditions that are established within a building exchange energies with the outside climate. In a perfectly isolated inside, there would be no such exchange. But a building, in this regard, is just like the rest of the earth as a weather system. Nature is always trying everywhere to equalize its energies, and so the building as an attempt to create climatic conditions unlike those of its surrounds is just one more barrier to overcome. Thus the skin of the building, the material that stands between interior and exterior climatic conditions, is always being driven by nature to exchange heat energies. It does this through conduction, the process in which molecules transfer heat energies one to the other; through convection, the process in which currents of air flow from higher to lower climatic energy states; and through radiation, the process in which heat energies are exchanged directly with other bodies that are at different temperatures. The rates at which these flows of heat are encouraged or discouraged are a function of the heat-conducting characteristics of the materials placed between the interior and exterior climatic conditions and the differences between interior and exterior temperatures. The rates of these interchanges become a basis, when combined with the information of the bioclimatic chart, to determine how much heat energy must be added or subtracted from the interior air to maintain comfort conditions.

The third measure that mechanical engineers use in attempting to provide building inhabitants with conditions of interior climatic comfort is the efficiency with which different machines convert fuel to the form of energy necessary to maintain comfort in a building. A fireplace chemically liberates the potential heat energy of wood in a way that makes approximately 20 percent of this energy available to heat a building. A cast-iron stove can increase this efficiency to 40 percent. A modern natural gas furnace can accomplish this task when operating at peak efficiencies at 96 percent. Cooling, humidifying or dehumidifying, and ventilating a building all involve the use of machines that have similar kinds of efficiencies in the conversion of fuel into useful forms of climate-modifying energy.

The job of the mechanical engineer is thus to understand the climatic stress placed on a building, including those times when climatic conditions outside are least conducive to human comfort inside, as well as the thermal loads placed on buildings by all its heat-producing as well as heat-dissipating elements including people, machinery, lighting, and the building skin, and then to select climate-modifying machines that convert inside climatic conditions to those of the comfort zone at the maximum efficiency and lowest cost.

CLIMATE MAPPED AS FELT FORCE

Climate as felt force has always been sensed by people in how it touches their skin. Before there was the flow of British thermal units from higher to lower energy states there was the touch of air that was cold or warm, damp or dry, moving or still. It is this difference that expresses the condition of being alive. It is this sense of touch that protects us when we are held, warms us when we are covered. Each kind of holding creates a boundary that locates people in the

How the climate
is actually felt by
the human body
cannot be reduced
to numbers.

natural world. Each kind of boundary creates an idea of where and how people are in that world. The first climatic boundary was that of the clearing, the second the garden, the third the boundary of the porch. Then came the enclosure of the dwelling itself with its difference between the corner and the middle of the external wall and between the floor and the ceiling of a room. Within these boundaries exists an even finer definition of place as climate that includes the hearth, the bed, clothing, and skin. In each case it is the boundary as the place between two climatic worlds that allows human beings to know that they are alive.

Architectural Technology as an Expression of the Map of Nature as Felt Force

Felt natural force in architecture is expressed as the material form of the frame, the weather envelope, and the openings of a building. Each of these forms contains the scientific definition of the natural phenomena that it modifies as well as the accretion of empirical knowledge that has been collected by engineering over the course of history that specifies how building materials perform tasks. But the expression of this knowledge that is manipulated by architects and is inhabited by people is found in the primordial set of forms that these forces take when they are constructed. These forms act as a seminal outline of a symbolic definition of natural force that allows the force to be interpreted as a significant manifestation of the place of people in nature.

GRAVITY AS FELT FORCE IN THE STRUCTURAL FRAME

Architecture has been organized around the need to redirect gravity since human beings first constructed permanent buildings. The earliest ruins of Stone Age pit houses have left behind clear markings in

The climate surrounds us in the air as it surrounds this teahouse in Katsura.

the form of four stones hollowed out to receive four wooden posts that in turn supported four beams and a roof. The architectural frame has taken on a number of shapes over the course of architectural history depending on the material that it was constructed of. These shapes separate generally into those that derive from trees and the characteristics of wood as a structural material and those that derive from stone and its characteristics as a structural material. Iron, steel, and reinforced concrete have changed the magnitude of spans that can be achieved and have reduced the amount of material required to do so because they have greater capacities to resist bending and shear, but the essential form of the wood frame that was evidenced in the first pit house or the stone wall of a burial mound has remained conceptually unchanged.

Gravity as felt force is manifest in building frames as *the rooted order of the earth*. The frame translates the perceived qualities of gravity's regularity into conceptions of repetitive pattern and permanence. The architectural frame at once defines the structure of the world of natural force to be orderly and that of human residence to be the same.

SUNLIGHT AS FELT FORCE IN THE WINDOW

Architectural sunlight is a much different matter than an electrical engineer's concerns for illuminating a building. This is not to say that all of the task-oriented concerns of the lighting engineer are unimportant to architects; rather, it is an issue of the dual use of light in buildings. One of these uses is to perform tasks. Adherents of the point of view contend that light was first introduced in buildings to accomplish utilitarian ends and should remain so. But a second task of sunlight is to illuminate the forms that make up the structure itself and to link these forms with those of the building's and thus the inhabitants' context. This nonutilitarian use of light establishes the character of a place rather than the visual capacity to perform a task in that space. The sun is the source of choice of light to architects for all the reasons that it is objectionable to engineers. The sun contributes an ingredient to architectural form that binds the whole together in a never ending range of subtle variations. Its directionality gives these objects shape and form in the dimensions it creates as the unevenness of reflection of surfaces that see the sun from different orientations. It gives texture and color to these surfaces as their material characteristics vary. It places all objects in relation

The regular, permanent, and progressively smaller section of
Exeter's brick columns as they grow higher manifests gravity as the
rooted order of the earth.

to one another so that the organization of the whole might be perceived. It allows parts to be referenced by the whole just as it allows them to come together to form it. The sun delivers a sense of time to these objects as it passes from horizon to horizon. Architectural forms come into being as the sun rises and die each evening as the sun sets. Openings in the envelopes of buildings transmit all these possibilities into the domain that human beings inhabit. The interior of buildings is given character in the infinite variety that natural light is able to deliver. The simple origin of architectural light is in a moving sun, a cloudy or clear sky, and the shape and placement of an opening in relation to a surface that reflects light; and the reflective characteristics of the surface itself can be combined in ways that are as luminescent, rich, and powerfully moving as are found in a French Gothic cathedral or as mundane and flat as those found in a contemporary commercial office building.

Sunlight as felt force is manifest in the window as *that which gathers all things into the human domain.* The boundary of the human domain is the horizon as the farthest reach of sight. All things are given their name and place, including buildings, by sunlight. The electric light of the night serves only to confirm the reduction in the scope and ability of artificial illumination to place things in time and space. Electric light is a little world without reference to the cosmos. It is a tiny luminescent island in comparison to the breadth and depth of the ideas that sunlight gathers into our domain.

CLIMATE AS FELT FORCE IN THE WEATHER ENVELOPE

The architectural form that the modification of climate takes is that of the weather envelope. The weather envelope comprises the material elements of architecture that stand between the inside and the outside climate. They are the floor, the walls, the ceiling, and the roof of the building. These forms have been familiar to house inhabitants since human beings first constructed houses. Floors were made to insulate the dwelling from the moisture and cold of the ground. Walls and ceilings were made to enclose the space from inclement conditions outside. And the roof was made to shed moisture. These utilitarian boundaries quickly gained the symbolic status associated with the separation of the inside from the outside. The inside of a domain became synonymous with all the values associated with home. The outside remained primarily the domain in which nature reigned supreme. The relationship between the two was nested layers

This moon door in a Chinese garden acts as a window that gathers all things into the human domain.

of insideness created by changes in climatic boundaries. Fireplaces often become a companion to the weather envelope as a means to convert solar energy that has been stored in the summer in trees into useful winter heat. As a definition of insideness, the hearth may be the oldest of architectural technologies. It established a thermal place of gathering before other technological elements of architecture had been invented.

Climate as felt force is manifest in the weather envelope of a building as *the boundary of touch*. It is all the sensual ways in which people are placed in relation to the qualities of the air as the product of hearing, smelling, and feeling. The boundary of touch defines the climate to be a coinhabitant of the human occupation of nature. The air alone among the natural forces tangibly penetrates the boundary of the human body as breath.

Technological Form in Architecture and the Three Maps of Nature

Science has attempted to describe the physical forces of nature under the two fundamental headings of matter and energy, which, in turn, are interchangeable. From this commonality spring the separate laws of mechanics as the underpinning of architectural structure, thermodynamics as the underpinning of architectural enclosure, and optics as the underpinning of architectural illumination. This summation has produced an extremely concise, empirically demonstrable, and numerically predictable view of nature as human context. Engineering benefits from the legitimateness of this viewpoint not so much in the methods it prescribes to arrive at utilitarian solutions but in its common vision of nature as the sum of its empirical performance.

Technological form in architecture need not cease to conform to the laws of mathematical nature to accept other meanings in human existence. Other activities of human significance take place in a world of empirical force that does not prevent them from being understood in ways that are fitting to the kind of ideas that they intend to create. Architectural technology is not a function of its literal prowess alone. It intends to create symbolic associations that locate people in nature in ways that are not simply the literal outcomes of its mechanical performance. These associations are at least as important to the ways that human beings understand and reside in nature as are their more pragmatic counterparts. There is little evidence that the first hut was not attended by a myth of protection, that the

The boundary of touch is made manifest each time a construction creates a distinction in how we feel that which envelops us. Photograph of Dutch farmhouse by Simon Beason.

first fire was not attended by thoughts of control, and that the first lashed tree branches did not carry with them the nascent conception of pattern. Words such as "protection," "control," and "pattern" are human constructs that stem from the tangible manipulation of a palpable natural world. They transcend that physicality to become ideas that attempt to bring mental order to self-conscious thoughts that attend these manipulations. The construct of utility as empirical fact is the myth of engineering. It has many competitors.

The depth and power of science as a definer of natural force requires that technological form in architecture be given specific voice if architectural technology is to present an alternative underlying structure to that of engineering. It is important not that these definitions are considered more humanly authentic than those of science but rather that they allow thought concerning technology to proceed along different lines than those of engineering. This is in no way to demean the contributions that engineering has made to the construction of buildings. The buildings of the twentieth century are vastly different from those of the eighteenth century because of the knowledge that engineering has brought to architecture. If, however, the relationship of people to nature that is forged through technology is not to be limited to the explicit value of engineering as utility alone, then architects must assume responsibility for contributing a metaphorical understanding of technology in design that engineers are unable to provide but that remains an issue of human significance. To do so they must reformulate the definition of natural force, not to be inconsistent with the empirical knowledge of engineering, but to be more consistent with the way in which technology is humanly inhabited by body, mind, and spirit.

Part II

■

Mechanics and Meaning in Four Houses

5. Finnish Log Farmhouse

Background

The Finnish farmhouse examined in this chapter was originally constructed in Konginkangas, central Finland, in 1860. A very similar building constructed in 1844 in the same area was brought to the Seurasaari Open Air Museum in Helsinki in 1909. With the exception of the shake rather than sod roof, the chimney, which was introduced in Finland in the eighteenth century, and the glass windows, which are a nineteenth-century addition to the form of this house, it has changed little over the course of nine hundred years. Its predecessors were initiated around the time of Christ when the Finnish peoples first began to migrate to this part of Europe from the southeast. As these people drove the native Lapps farther north, they brought with them the traditions of wood building that covered a broad band of the Northern Hemisphere extending from Japan through China and Eastern Europe to northern Germany and Scandinavia. The building tradition of these areas was that of wood rather than of stone as it was farther south.

There is speculation that this first Finnish farmhouse was a sauna, the place where Finns traditionally bathe. An early example of a Finnish dwelling was a pit house with a wooden roof that was covered with sod or birch bark. It contained a stone fireplace and perhaps had a single small shuttered opening besides the wooden door but little else. Its successor was a crude, single-room wooden-frame sod-covered house that was built totally above ground. Again this single room contained a chimneyless hearth and perhaps was lit by a

The farmhouse is from the state of Konginkangas, in the center of Finland, at 64 degrees north latitude.

small shuttered opening but was otherwise very stark. As ingenuity and wealth allowed the time and knowledge to construct log walls, successive houses became technologically more sophisticated. Stone foundations were added to the construction, as was a chimney for the hearth. The contemporary configuration of the house, with a main room, entry hall, storage room, and guest room with a chimneyed fireplace and glass windows, emerged in Finland during the late eighteenth century.

Finland was a country that was slow to adopt the tools and ideas of the industrial revolution. This peninsular country lies at the edge of European civilization and thus did not come into early contact with the products of that civilization. The western part of the country differs somewhat from the eastern part in this regard, as this part of Finland has been historically dominated by Sweden and thus reflects Swedish culture. The east has been dominated by Russian Slavic culture and has therefore lagged behind the west in developing technology and wealth. In the east slash-and-burn farming persisted well into the twentieth century, as did the use of the wooden plow. In the west, technological goods such as clocks became prevalent, at least among the wealthy, in the nineteenth century. An examination of a nineteenth-century farmhouse in the middle of Finland is therefore a little like looking back hundreds of years into European history. Little changed in the lives of most Finnish farmers over these nine hundred years until relatively recently.

Of the four houses included in this study, only this one qualifies as vernacular architecture. It is not the product of a class of design specialists called architects but rather was designed by the people who made and lived in it. This is a kind of culturally housed design skill and knowledge that has largely disappeared in contemporary industrial societies. It represents a method of trial-and-error learning about natural forces that has characterized the traditional development of technology. As technical construction lessons are painfully learned, they become encoded in the cultural rituals of making a house. When new modifications are demonstrated to be desirable in this design, they become woven into this legacy. A relatively steep learning curve characterizes early fundamental construction choices and then slows as viable solutions are achieved and few new technological possibilities present themselves in these cultures.

Description of the Building

SITE AND PLAN

The living area of the log farmhouse is a simple rectangular box, 23 feet wide by 28 feet long. It was normally part of a larger building, but the rooms of that structure were only to be occupied temporarily by guests or used as storage. All the members of the family and all of the farm helpers lived in the single large room of the farmhouse, as they would have done in a medieval manor house. The bench around the perimeter of the room provided a sleeping place for each individual and storage for what must have been a meager number of personal belongings. A spinning wheel normally occupied the place of best natural interior light, and a small cupboard held the family's prize possessions. A large stone hearth occupied an entire corner of the room and provided the social as well as functional center of the house, particularly during the cold, dark winter months. In the short summer, all attention turned to planting, tending, and harvesting the crops that ensured survival through the next winter.

The site of the farmhouse is a traditional eighteenth-century Finnish farmyard. This farmyard is created by an array of loosely organized outbuildings around an open space. They include the main house itself, which may or may not be attached to the sauna and storage rooms, the sauna if detached, a cooking shelter, a stable, a toolshed, a net barn, other barns, and a boathouse. Tighter organizations of connected buildings were relatively rare in Finland. In the winter, cooking, eating, sleeping, and light work all were carried out in the main room. In the summer, the work was in the fields, cooking was done in a separate shed, and family and farmhands slept in the out-buildings. This

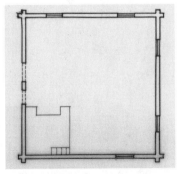

The plan of the farmhouse is a 23'x 28' space with a large fireplace in one corner.

Though more than one room was often constructed in these farmhouses, only one of these rooms was occupied by the farm family and the farm laborers.

annual migration recorded changes in the Finnish climate as concentrated and dispersed places of human habitation.

CLIMATE AND SUNLIGHT

The climate of Finland depends on two major conditions. The first is that the country is the northernmost in the world, extending from 60 to 70 degrees north latitude. This far north location would suggest extremely harsh climatic conditions were it not for the relatively warm temperatures of the currents of the Atlantic Ocean. Westerly winds bring these moderating temperatures and moisture across the country. Even with these moderating influences, however, the temperatures of Finland would not encourage any but the most hardy of souls to migrate there. Winter mean temperatures are approximately 20 degrees Fahrenheit in February. Extreme winter low temperatures might reach -33 degrees Fahrenheit, and average low temperatures in this part of Finland are 12 degrees Fahrenheit. Spring begins at the end of May, when mean temperatures rise to

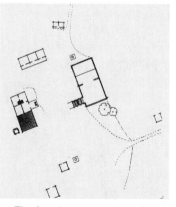

The farmhouse was sited with a barn, a sauna, and an array of other outbuildings to loosely form a farmyard. Site drawing by Andrzej Piotrowski.

between 32 and 50 degrees Fahrenheit. Summer, which is defined as a mean temperature above 50 degrees Fahrenheit, begins sometime in June and lasts until late August. Maximum temperatures do not exceed 72 degrees Fahrenheit during this season. Fall mean temperatures are moderate, and this season may be extended into early November by warm oceanic winds from the West. The relative humidity of the country varies from 86 to 92 percent in the winter to 65 to 70 percent in the summer.

Winter is a formidable climatic issue in Finland. The country is a small thermal island that would otherwise be surrounded by ice-filled water and would be unable to sustain crops if not for the ocean currents that warm it. This anomaly can be traced in the tree and ice line that circumscribes the North Pole. This line is deeply eroded by the bodies of water that bound the west coast of Finland and moderate its temperatures.

The importance of climatic distinctions in the winter is recorded in the number of words that Finnish farmers use to describe changes in this season. The beginning of winter, November and December, is called autumn winter *(systalvi)*; January and February are called high winter *(keskitalvi)*; and March and April are called

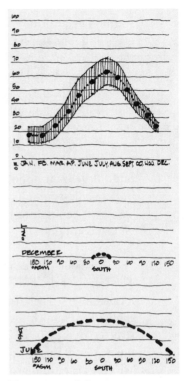

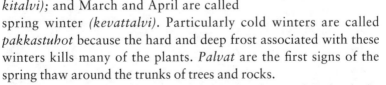

The average daily temperature in this part of Finland is 7°F in January, 28°F in May, 59°F in July, and 32°F in October. The duration of daylight and solar elevation at noon vary from approximately 3 hours with a maximum solar elevation of 4 degrees in January to 21 hours with an elevation of 50 degrees in June.

spring winter *(kevattalvi)*. Particularly cold winters are called *pakkastuhot* because the hard and deep frost associated with these winters kills many of the plants. *Palvat* are the first signs of the spring thaw around the trunks of trees and rocks.

Because of the extreme north location of central Finland, the difference in the amount of sunlight received varies greatly from summer to winter. On December at 65 degrees north latitude the sun rises at 15 degrees east of south and sets at 15 degrees west of south. The altitude that the sun reaches on December 21 is 4 degrees at noon. The sun is thus little more than a brief illumination of the horizon in midwinter at this northern latitude. This lack of sunlight is exacerbated by the extreme cloudiness of Finland in the winter. From October to January there are normally only one to three cloudless days a month. The winter is characterized by 70 to 80 percent cloudy skies whereas in the summer skies are cloudy 50 to 60 percent of the time. The summer is the time of the midnight sun. On June 21 the sun rises at 155 degrees east of south, rises to an altitude of 50 degrees at noon, and sets at 155 degrees west of south. Thus in the coldest months of December, January, and February there is very little sunlight to be had, whereas in the moderate summer it is almost constant.

The Mechanics of Technological Form

The frame of the Finnish log farmhouse is made from the trunks of local conifers. These trees grow straight and tall as they compete for sunlight in Finnish forests. The bearing walls of the house are constructed of logs 10 to 20 inches in diameter that have been cut from the trunks of these conifers. The problem with these logs is that they are very heavy and generally round in section. Neither of these characteristics suggests easy ways of assembling the logs to create a ver-

The Finnish log farmhouse reorganizes trees, stones, and earth to suit human purpose.

tical wall. The solution to this problem, developed by the wood craftsmen of northern Europe, was to notch the ends of each log to receive a second log of similar dimension that had been laid perpendicular to it and notched in the same manner. Thus by placing alternating layers of notched logs perpendicular to one another, each log would act as a buttress to the log that received it and in turn would be buttressed by it so that they could no longer roll off the log below them. As logs were stacked by alternating the thick and more narrow diameter of the tree trunk, a roughly even vertical surface could be built up by rolling logs up inclined planes into place. When this process was repeated at the unsupported ends of the logs, the four walls of a rectangular space were created. The resultant technological form was that of a box comprising four orthogonal thick wooden bearing walls. The superstructure of the heavy timber beams of the roof sat atop these walls.

The roof of the farmhouse was required to span a large distance to create the singular space of the living area of the farmhouse. The loads that the superstructure of the roof were required to carry were large both because the weight of the materials used to construct the roof were heavy in themselves and because the weight of the snow that would accumulate on the roof in the winter was great. The tradition of covering the roof with sod carried over from previous farmhouse construction. The root structure of the grasses that grew in the sod created a multilayered series of channels that guided moisture down the slope of the roof to the eaves, where it ran off and onto the earth. The ability of the sod to continue to perform this task was ensured because the grasses of the upper layer of sod were kept alive with the nutrients of the earth that surrounded the roots and the water that they were intended to shed. Later, lapped birch bark was substituted for the heavier sod.

Both forms of shingles are fairly effective at shedding moisture, but neither has the ability to span large distances. Both must be supported at close intervals by a series of small-diameter branches called purlins that gather the weight of the sod or birch bark and the moisture that they carry to a series of perpendicular branches slightly larger in diameter called rafters that are spaced at wider intervals. These rafters are supported by a major longitudinal beam at the midpoint between the wall and the peak of the farmhouse roof, where they are most vulnerable to bending.

The superstructure of the roof and ceiling, which must span a distance of 23 feet, consists of a large beam, 16 inches deep, that bisects the 28-foot dimension of the farmhouse living space. Atop this beam sit three evenly spaced 14-inch-deep beams that run perpendicular to the first beam. This second set of smaller beams divides each of the 14-foot spans created by the first beam into four 5-foot, 9-inch spans. Both sets of beams are anchored to the bearing log walls with the same notched joint that connects wall members. The outer two secondary beams support similarly sized beams that run above them on short posts. These beams support branch roof rafters that are spaced at 12-inch intervals. Above these are boards or branches that are smaller in diameter and commensurably more closely spaced that run perpendicular to the rafters. Finally, the sod or birch bark of the roof rests on these boards.

Supporting the roof at its quarter points instead of at the center ridge makes good mechanical sense. If the roof were supported by the log walls and a single beam and king post at the ridge, one-half of the weight of the roof structure would bear on the center of the major beam that spans 23 feet. This would place a good deal of weight on this beam where it is most susceptible to failure in bending. By moving this weight out to the quarter points, the weight that it supports is borne closer to a bearing wall, making the beam below less likely to fail in bending.

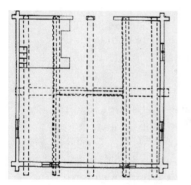

A 16" deep beam spans the 23' dimension of the room below. Resting on it are five perpendicular beams that divide the 12'6" spans created by the primary beam into four equal spatial divisions of 5'9" each.

The weather envelope of the building is designed to protect the interior of the farmhouse from the winter cold. The walls are made up of 10- to 20-inch-diameter logs that, when dry, have an R-value of 18 (average resistance to heat flow). This compares to an only slightly greater R-value of 21 for a contemporary insulated 2-by-6-inch stud cavity wall. As the log walls of the farmhouse dry, a cellular structure of small air pockets is left behind that makes this dry timber a good source of insulation. The ceiling and floor of the farmhouse are both insulated from ambient air temperatures by dry earth. An air space is created above the ceiling and below the roof of the farmhouse. This space is sealed at the edges with dry soil. The weight of

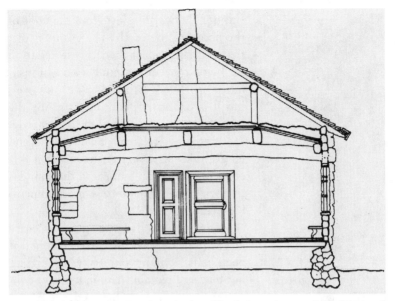

The gathering and transfer of gravitational loads from the covering of the roof to log walls and to the earth are recorded in the organization and size of elements of the section of the farmhouse. Section drawing by Andrzej Piotrowski.

earth at the edge of the ceiling might seem impracticable in terms of conventional wisdom, but the problem of providing support for the roof of a log house is far easier to solve than it is to prevent the heat loss that would occur in this area. It is both the place where the ceiling meets the wall (and hence is prone to exfiltration at the joint) and the place where the air space is able to offer the least thermal protection to the interior of the house. The dry earth that naturally settles into the crevice created by the juncture of the roof and ceiling helps to solve both the conductive and the convective heat loss problem that would otherwise occur at this joint.

A second air space is the pocket between the earth and the floor created by the 2-foot-thick stone foundation walls that mark the perimeter of the dwelling. Earth is piled up around the inside of these stone walls to both insulate the stone which transmits heat effectively and to seal the log wall/stone foundation juncture against the high infiltration rates as at the ceiling/wall juncture. Heat lost through the 3-inch-thick hand-sawed floorboards is trapped and held in this dead air space momentarily, keeping the air below the floor warmer than it might otherwise be. The ground below this space also retains some of this heat and hence provides a small heat

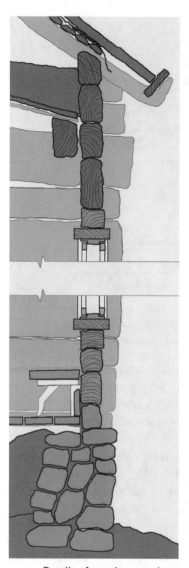

Details of weather envelope closure at the floor and ceiling. Wall section by Andrzej Piotrowski.

sink for the warmth lost from the floor of the house to the earth. The granular dirt that is piled against the stone foundation wall would become a poor source of insulation if it were allowed to become wet, but it is protected from moisture by the stone foundation wall and the floor above. Dry earth has a relatively high R-value, and its granular structure ensures that it fills cracks between the floor and the foundation wall where the house is most vulnerable to infiltration.

The windows of the farmhouse are larger than they would have been had it been constructed even fifty years earlier, but they still remain small in terms of contemporary houses. The predecessors to these windows were 1-foot-square openings that were closed by wooden shutters when it was dark out and covered with an oilcloth during sunlit hours. These openings were so small because the window constituted a thermal wound in the wall in the winter. In January, when temperatures are among the coldest in Finland, these openings would provide only 12 hours of light a month, or an average of 25 minutes of sunlight per day. In return, the oilcloth spread across this 1-foot-square opening would lose as much heat as 40 square feet of an adjacent 15-inch-thick log wall. That means that every opening for light requires forty times the amount of wood to be burned to maintain internal thermal comfort as would an equal amount of log wall. This requirement translates into forty times the time and effort required to cut, split, and stack firewood to support this opening thermally and forty times the amount of forest acreage necessary to support this use of firewood. The glass windows that replaced the oilcloth were, of course, considerably more

The windows of this nineteenth-century farmhouse are much larger than those of earlier farmhouses, but they are still relatively small in relation to the size of the room they are intended to illuminate.

energy efficient, but not enough so to warrant large windows. They still lose as much heat as 20 square feet of 15-inch-thick log wall. The five 3-by-5-foot windows of the study house transmit nearly three times the amount of heat, as do all the log walls that surround them. In return, these windows admit light deeply into the interior of the farmhouse.

This light is reflected primarily by the wood floor of the farmhouse, giving the interior a warm, diffuse glow when the sun shines. It must have been considered to be of great value to warrant their construction. During the winter months, when light would be most valuable, it was least available. November (12 hours), December (8 hours), January (12 hours), and February (45 hours) each has only a few daylight hours on either side of noon. The little sunlight that the windows transmit during the winter provided a special place at the edge of the dwelling to do chores that demanded above-average luminescent conditions. Spinning wool, weaving, and reading might number among these tasks.

Analysis of Technological Form
THE LEGACY OF THE NOTCHED LOG WALL

The notch that allows round logs to be piled one atop the other to form a wall is a uniquely human invention. It is an ingenious

Trees growing in a forest manifest organic form, an organization that seeds, soil, sunlight, and water promote.

response to the need to transform a natural resource into humanly useful form. In this transformation lies the power of the human hand and the human mind to modify the resources of the natural world in ways that allow those resources to acquire a shape capable of defying the problems that nature presents to human survival. Nature is both the source of the problem and the resource to solve that problem. Nature creates the climate that threatens human survival during the long, harsh winter, and gravity makes enclosing a heavy timber space from this climate such a challenging task. Nature also provides the possibilities to accomplish protection from the climate in the trees, stones, and earth that can be found on the site. Technology is the act of learning to reassemble these possibilities in ways that overcome the difficulties that nature presents.

The human invention that promotes this reassembly in the Finnish log farmhouse is the notched joint. Round logs do not sit easily or stably atop one another. Resisting the natural desire of a log to roll off the log below it with a long lever arm that counters this torque must have been a hard-fought intellectual and physical battle. One imagines that it began with the simpler piling up of unnotched perpendicular logs to form a rectangular space like the structures that are used as traditional Finnish crop storage buildings. The problem was then to develop a system of joinery that eliminated the spaces between alternating layers of logs while reinforcing the capacity of the walls to bear the great weight of the roof. The notch that lets one log down into its perpendicular partner so that the gap between succeeding logs might disappear was born of this need. Thus in the invention of this notch, the log is allowed to become a wall able to separate an inside from an outside climate.

The trunk of the tree in this wall remains recognizable as the tree albeit as a horizontal rather than vertical form. The notched joint that allows this form to come into being is fashioned with simple hand tools, so that the rudiments of this process are easy to men-

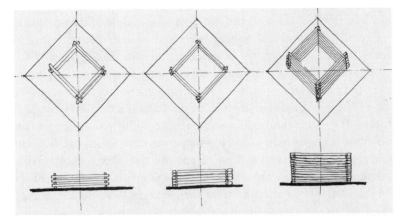

Organic order is transformed into rational order by felling and stacking
unnotched logs, as in the Finnish granary, and then by notching the logs,
as in the farmhouse.

tally grasp. Pieces of the construction are assembled in a manner that leaves a clear formal history of this process. The transformation of natural into manufactured form is graphically recorded in the process.

The notched log is at once a simple and a sophisticated solution to
the gapped layering of logs of the granary. By letting a log into its
perpendicular partner, problems of structural stability and of thermal
closure are simultaneously solved. Photograph by Simon Beason.

The notched joint, in this sense, is an example of the condition required to make all natural resources available to the possibility of reuse for human purpose. As this transformation is physically accomplished, it initiates a mental conception of order that originates with the purposeful reorganization of the material. The tree growing in the forest exhibits the pattern bequeathed to it by biological forces. It grows where soil, water, and sunlight make that growth possible. It grows to be as tall as competing trees will allow. Its form and organization are thus the outcome of a complex web of organic relationships that govern where and how plants survive and prosper on the earth. The pattern of trees that emerges from the log wall of the Finnish farmhouse is an altogether different matter. It begins with the tree's felling, which divorces it from its natural biological order. The notch that allows these trees to be piled up to form a wall is the outcome of what the wall needs to accomplish as well as prefiguring the specific kinds of organization that individual logs might assume in becoming that wall. The orthogonal form that is the outcome of this process is inherent in the notch. The notch does not demand a right-angled order, but it gives preference to it. The form that results connotes a meaning not inherent in the act of this assembly alone; a wall denotes a specific human concept of something that encloses. This shift in organization, which is accompanied by a parallel shift in meaning, is equally true of the act of piling up stones to make a hearth or foundation wall, of assembling logs to create a roof superstructure, or of relocating sod to shed water from the roof.

Span is related to number and depth of spanning elements creating a hierarchical formal order, as is manifest by the underside of the farmhouse roof.

GRAVITY AND THE CONCEPTION OF HIERARCHICAL ORDER

The regularity of the size and spacing of roof members of the farmhouse is a manifestation of the uniformity of gravity. The purlins are evenly spaced at 4-inch intervals, creating with the rafters that support them at 12-inch intervals a uniform web of elements that gather the uniformly dispersed weight of the roofing material and moisture that it sheds. As each successive roof element spans a progressively larger distance, it is asked to gather a progressively larger share of the uniform weight of gravity and hence must become larger in section to do so. Each division of the space to be spanned is done so with elements of the superstructure that divide the space below into even geometric portions. The first beam cuts the space in half, the second set of beams cuts these halves into quarters, and the rafters subdivide the surface of the roof into equal 12-inch increments. The resultant form creates a pattern of hierarchical size in which section and length of roof members are inexorably linked to the uniformness of gravity. The progression of size and space between these elements is geometrically proportional to the weight they carry in carving out the space of the room below. Trial-and-error construction in the face of the uniform pull of gravity creates a complex formal pattern that relates the spanning characteristics of material to amounts of weight and to relative distances. The exposed roof of a building almost always elicits a kind of human satisfaction that is due to its manifestation of the characteristic uniformity of gravity. Unlike walls or columns, it is in the spanning of space that this regularity is revealed to become a part of the human vocabulary of what constitutes order.

THE RESIDUAL RIDGE BEAM

In the center of the ceiling of the farmhouse is a log that is far too large in diameter for the task it performs. This log runs directly down the center of the space below but carries only the relatively minor weight of the ceiling boards that it helps to support. Its size and location cannot be functionally rationalized. It is a residue of the historic bifurcation of a house by its ridge beam. The ridge beam has traditionally marked the center of the roof so that space below might be spanned and moisture shed, and in so doing, this beam has often come to mark the social and sometimes spiritual center of the interior of the house. In many cultures, this line has taken on a special significance as the place in the house nearest to the heavens as it centers

The central longitudinal "residual" secondary beam.

life below. The superstructure of the Finnish farmhouse roof elimi-
nates the necessity of this ridge beam, as the weight of the roof
rafters is gathered at the quarter points of the span. The large ridge
beam that runs down the center of the house is thus a memory of
this once structurally necessary beam that has come to have its own
symbolic life.

THE RAISED FLOOR

The stone foundation of the farmhouse separates the interior living space from the cold and dampness of the earth below but in so
doing elevates the floor of the structure above the ground. This is
not a trivial relocation in terms of its relation either to the remainder of the living world or to the experience of the farm's inhabitants.
Trees, grasses, crops, domestic animals, and wild animals all inhabit
the surface of the earth. They are all tied to the earth by gravity, by
the abundance that the soil provides, and by their inability to mentally or physically conceive of their place of residence as being elsewhere. The earth spreads out in all horizontal directions as their
floor but may not be vertically modified. Early humans were similarly attached to this surface. A residence might be created in a
natural clearing on a somewhat level and well-drained piece of land,
or land might be intentionally leveled and cleared for this purpose.

Raising the floor from the ground isolates inhabitants from the
cold and damp of the earth. Photograph by Simon Beason.

In either case, the floor of the dwelling remained on the ground. In rising above the earth as a tool that separates humans from the discomfort of cold and wet, the new ground of inhabitation elevates this tiny abode of human beings mentally above that of other forms of life. This distinction of separation will henceforth serve to define the relationship of a dwelling to its surroundings. To locate this floor at grade will be to participate directly in nature while successively greater elevation above that surface will be to signify an intellectual as well as social distance from nature's ground and all that ground connotes. The human mind is reminded by the weight of the human body of this distinction each time a person ascends stairs to enter the farmhouse.

THE THICK LOG WALL

The walls of the Finnish log farmhouse might have been made of a very thin material that provided even better thermal protection from the bitter cold of the winter at 65 degrees north latitude than do the thick log walls. However, they would remain far less emotionally satisfying even in their improved mechanical performance if they were to be constructed of such a material. A metaphorical human mind connects thickness with strength. The thicker the wall, the more protection it might offer from any threat. On a cold winter night, it is possible to crawl into a bed that has been preheated by a thin, light electric blanket, but there is never the same sense of protection gleaned from this electrical warmth as attends wiggling warm feet down into the cold space covered by heavy blankets or a thick down comforter. It is not the mechanics of the transfer of heat in this bed that become the basis for the sense of thermal protection but rather its analogue as a physical dimension. The felt thickness of the wall becomes the thought of protection from external danger. The small openings in this wall as deep recesses only serve to reinforce this notion of being enclosed by a heavy, thick coat. There are few openings in this surface because these openings make inhabitants vulnerable to threats from outside.

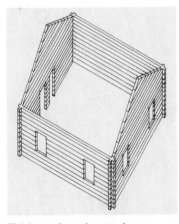

Thickness is understood as protection in the log wall.

THE CUPPED CEILING

As the boards of the ceiling slope downward to meet the long walls of the farmhouse to provide a place for the insulation for the soil above, they create a concave ceiling of the dwelling. This cupped shape denotes a conceptually different sense of being enclosed by the interior than would occur if it were either flat or upturned at the edge. A flat ceiling would connote the possibility of the infinite extension of the interior space. An upturned edge would mate the space along the wall with that of the outside rather than with the center of the house. The ceiling is a warm, wooden, low surface in the Finnish farmhouse that suggests that if continued, it would complete its own juncture with the earth much as an arch does. It thus delimits the space of the interior of the dwelling as the concave sky delimits the human domain on the earth. The world in both cases proceeds inward to a center that is created by what encloses people from a potentially infinite expanse. To be covered from the sky by a form that is reminiscent of that sky is to be metaphorically reconnected with the way in which people understand the limits of the natural world.

THE HEARTH AS THE CENTER OF THE DOMAIN

The interior of the weather envelope of the farmhouse is warmed in the winter by a great stone hearth that occupies an entire corner of

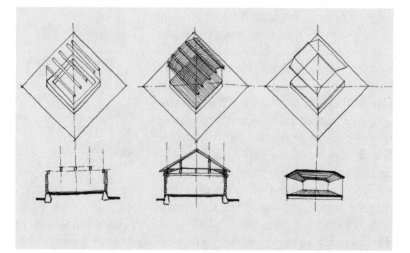

The cupped ceiling of the farmhouse provides a space at its edges for insulating earth above while containing the space of the hearth below.

the dwelling. This massive stone construction serves as the place where all winter cooking is done as well as serving as the primary source of heat for the house in the winter. Its great size is due to the need to store the heat of the very hot flame that is the result of burning wood. Although the tip of a wood-burning flame may reach 2,300 degrees Fahrenheit, the space heat needs of building inhabitants are only 65 degrees Fahrenheit. If the heat of the flame was not stored in some manner, the vast majority of this thermal disparity between heat source and heat need would go up the chimney. The stone of the fireplace has a relatively large capacity to store heat for future use. As wood is burned in the hearth for cooking meals or for space heating during the day, a portion of this heat is absorbed by the rock that surrounds it. This process serves both to even out the heat that is distributed while the fire is lit and to reradiate heat that is stored in the stone when the fire goes out at night, transferring daytime excess heat into nighttime warmth.

This warmth is not at the geometric center of the farmhouse, but it becomes the social center of the dwelling as it gathers inhabitants around it. The sheer size of the hearth would ensure that it would become the most prominent of Finnish household furnishings, but it is not size alone that creates the significance of this construction. The opening of the hearth is at its interior corner. A circle

The hearth and bed adjacent to, or on top of, its stone mass suggest a place where the family cares for its vulnerable members.

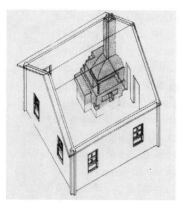

The hearth gathers house inhabitants into a circle that defines the center of the domain to be jointly its open flame and the people around it.

that includes this corner identifies the center of the farmhouse to be joint territory of the hearth and those who gather around it to cook or to be warmed. In the deep of winter there is almost no sunlight outside, so that this flame also becomes the luminescent center of the dwelling. If it is the thick coat of the floor that separates inhabitants from the ground, the walls that separate inhabitants from the air, and the ceiling that separates inhabitants from the sky, it is the hearth that forms the new center of this territory. This is a sensed thermal and luminescent center of heat and light amid the cold and dark of winter nights that redefines the center of human existence.

THE HEARTH AS A PLACE OF HUMAN CARE

The fireplace also serves as a special place for farm family members who might be particularly vulnerable to the stresses of a cold climate. There is a little stairway at the back of the hearth that allows the very young, the very old, or the sick to lie down on the warm rocks. This is not a place of everyday warmth as is the opening at the front of the hearth. It is, rather, a special place that represents the human ability to care for the well-being of a fellow. Unlike animals or hunter-gatherers, farmers could take action to prevent the weak from falling prey to natural enemies. This privileged thermal place on top of the hearth is symbolic of the human ability to care for the vulnerable among them instead of abandoning the weak to their Darwinian fate.

THE PRECIOUS WINDOW

The harsh winter climate made windows thermally "precious." The need to reestablish the link with the outside that had been severed by the opaque logs of the weather envelope was apparently greater than the cost of the heat that would be lost through this opening. These farmhouse windows represent the human need to reestablish a place of dwelling among the other forms of the natural world. Their transparent surfaces frame a part of this world, no matter how small, so that it might be brought into the domain of the farmhouse. They capture a portion of the farmyard and all its activities, a small portion of the fields that nourish the farmers, and a small portion of the forest from which the farm was carved. Windows reconnect the interior of the farmhouse with the rhythms of sunlight that indicate the time of the year or of the day. This is the rhythm that animates and gives life to the outside world. The rhythms of sunlight were the rhythms of Finnish peasant life. It told farmers when to plow, when to plant, and when to harvest their crops. The sun told the time of animal births and the time to collect berries. Its cycles were the cycles of the life and death of the natural world as manifest in the seasons of the year and in the chronological age of farmhouse inhabitants. The window, no matter how small, connected the farmhouse to its land and the occupants of the farmhouse to the time and place of their existence.

THE RECIPROCITY OF THE HEARTH AND WINDOWS

The hearth at the thermal center of the farmhouse plays a reciprocal role with the windows as illumination. During the daylight hours of the spring, summer, and fall, the windows draw occupants to solitary tasks at the edge of the structure. At night and in the deep of winter, it is the fireplace that provides the light at the center of the farmhouse as it gathers inhabitants around its warmth. This kind of pushing out into the landscape followed by retreat into the protection of the center is common to cold climates. It mirrors a commensurate mental expansiveness and withdrawal that typifies climatic

A window, no matter what size, is a thermally expensive technology in this extremely harsh northern climate. The reward for its insertion must have proven worth its cost, because it remained a staple of log farmhouse design and grew in size as the wealth of the farmer allowed. Photograph by Simon Beason.

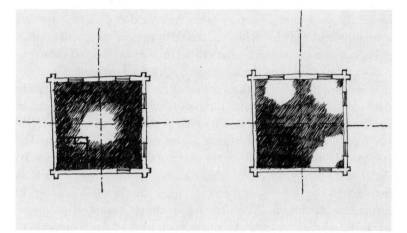

The reciprocity of the hearth and window must have been both seasonal and diurnal. The window would draw inhabitants to the edge of the house when the sun shone, and the hearth would draw them to its center in the darkness of long, cold winter nights.

social rituals of northern peoples. The spring is the time when heavy, warm clothing is set aside for lighter outerwear. There is a kind of emotional opening up during this season that gives thanks for the end of the always too long winter of confinement and the coming of warm temperatures and spring rains.

The fall, in contrast, is the beginning of the time of quiet. It is a time to withdraw from the activity of warmer months to begin a period of contemplation. Winter covers all in a blanket of soundless beauty. Summer brings forth the bounty of life. The fireplace refers to these rhythms of day and night and of seasons as it serves to complement the natural world that is invited into the house by the sunlight of the windows.

Technological Form as Metaphorical Thought
This mode of learning about the relationship between natural force and constructed form is direct and immediate. Trees are felled for construction, dragged from the forest, and stacked to dry. Their great weight is made tangible in this process and is reinforced when they are rolled up inclined planks to assemble walls. Spans are achieved by lifting heavy logs into place and having different sizes of logs report their capacity to perform the tasks to which they are being assigned. Succeeding structural members are placed by hand in accordance with the rules of construction. Walls are chinked by

hand to prevent drafts, and the hearth is piled up with mortared stone. The memory of cold winter drafts would promote a high standard of craft in accomplishing both of these tasks. Wood to heat the farmhouse during the winter must be chopped and stacked for future use. The severity of the winter is measured in cords of wood burned, just as the bounty of the summer growing season is measured in the amount of crops harvested. Every act has a direct consequence. Each is tangibly felt as it is performed. The knowledge of the natural world that is acquired is palpable. Abstractions of the structure of that world arise from these acts of the human hand.

METAPHORS OF TANGIBLE TRANSACTIONS

These technological responses suggest a kind of design thought in which invisible natural forces are manifest in technological forms in terms of how human beings might come to tangibly understand these forces. Like the contemporary activity of camping out in a tent, this direct and palpable experience seems to reunite people physically and mentally with natural phenomena in a way that is not made opaque by intervening mechanisms. There appears to be a kind of human joy associated with this tangible understanding of the use of material to respond to natural force. A notched log is, in this sense, more satisfying than a hidden metal tie bar, lighting a fire more satisfying than turning up a thermostat, and sliding open a wooden shutter more satisfying than switching on an electric light. Each of these activities can be felt as the outcome of the action of a human hand rather than as the more abstract outcome of the workings of a machine. Revealing the character of invisible natural force through forms that connote its palpable manipulation seems to reassure us that there is a fundamental ground for human experience. The abstract world of natural force coded in the even more abstract language of numbers begets an equally distant and abstract understanding of nature. These forces are made available to the human mind in the palpable technological forms of the Finnish log farmhouse.

This coupling of mechanics and meaning in the technological forms of the Finnish log farmhouse might be called *tangible transactions*. Tangible transactions create a set of formal metaphors that allow technology to be understood as the ideas of a literal reshaping of felt force. Felt force, in this instance, includes the felt harvesting of resources from nature, the ability to directly understand the modification of these resources to fulfill technological purpose as the felt action of hand tools, the felt form of these modifications as empathic with the way in which the human body would feel these same forces, and abstractions of inhabitation that grow directly from how these forms are felt by people. The floor of the house is able to connote a place above and distinct from other living things because people must lift the weight of their bodies to stand on it. The weight of the log walls as analogous to protection is felt by lifting them into place. The hearth is the center of the domain because its warmth can be felt, especially in contrast to the severe cold of the winter wind outside. The superstructure of the roof orders space because the ways in which it partitions that space originated from the frightening experience of structural failures. Light is a reminder of life because it is the way in which birth and death are noted. The amount of wood that is burned in the hearth is a direct measure of the severity of the winter as is felt in the labor of chopping and splitting logs.

Soon what each of these technologies does, and what it has come to mean in terms of the more general problem of human inhabitation, become blurred. The floor that separated from the cold and damp of the ground becomes the distinction of the human versus the natural domain; the notched log becomes the foundation of a notion of orthogonal human order; the relation of the size to span of roof members becomes the more complex notion of hierarchical order; the warmth of the hearth becomes the conception of center as gathering; and the light of the windows becomes the conception of time.

Nature becomes, to this kind of technological form, the ways in which these technological elements of the house give rise to a sensual definition of its forces. These forces are not considered to be the outcome of abstract definitions that provide a unified intellectual view of their origins. Nature is, in this sense, the accretion of forms that give meaning to the forces that they modify by taking on shapes and relationships that state the characteristics of these forces in ways that might be understood by the human body. Each new form defines a natural force as it places human beings within that force. Thick walls protect, a raised floor locates, the geometric pattern of the ceiling differentiates human from natural order, windows reconnect existence to natural rhythms, and the hearth centers. Each of these is a technological tool that has become an idea that finds its origin in that tool but transcends the literal and utilitarian meaning that might be assigned to it. To resist gravity with a geometric organization of spanning members may reflect the uniformity of gravity as the mechanical initiation of that form, but the conception of hierarchical order that might be interpreted from this organization of material is more than a mere extension of these mechanics. It is a conception of order that might only arise from placing wood in a manner that provokes the mental construct called pattern. The clearing of the farm centered by the farmyard, centered by the inside of the log room of the farmhouse, centered by the hearth, centered by the bed on top of the hearth, promotes an idea of thermal nesting that extends and deepens the conception of inside versus outside to include the notion of human care for the land and for one another. The light that gives life to all that exists in the farmer's domain forges the structure of the rhythm of life of the interior of this dwelling. Seasons personify human emotions that might be associated with a sense of birth, life, maturity, and death.

Technological metaphors of tangible transactions are less about what constitutes the primitive origins of architecture than about the human ability to understand the mechanics of natural force as a projection of ideas that emanate from the way in which those forces are directly experienced by the human mind and body.

6. Charles Moore House at Orinda

Background

Charles Moore was a young teacher at Berkeley when he and a group of students built this small house in 1962 in the relatively wealthy Bay Area community of Orinda, California. The house is part of a series of early Moore works in which he was feeling his way toward an architecture that was to take issue with the orthodox modern design sensibilities that prevailed at the time. This departure is given evidence by the fact that although the design won a Citation in Residential Design in the *Progressive Architecture* Ninth Annual Awards (1962), the jury showed their hesitance to condone design work that lay outside the conventions of modern orthodoxy by likening the plan to painting, and the interior to stage design. No comment could have provided a more apt springboard for the advent of postmodernism in the United States than this seemingly innocent caveat.

In 1962 the attack on modern design orthodoxy was gathering momentum. Robert Venturi wrote what was to become the manifesto of the movement, *Complexity and Contradiction in Architectural Form,* in that year. In this book, Venturi takes issue with what he sees as the shallow formalism of the modern movement as manifest in the inability of most of its later output either to stand up to rigorous intellectual criticism or to generate a kind and level of symbolic logic that would make such an analysis worthwhile. His call is to reinstate the intellectual depth of design thought in architecture. In the same year, Aldo Van Eyke's famous short treatise "Place and

Occasion," which mandated "making a welcome of every door and a countenance of every window," appeared in its first English translation. Van Eyke was as concerned with the modern movement's substitution of the metaphors of physics for those of the experiences of humanity as Venturi was with the intellectual turpitude that had overtaken contemporary architecture. His quest was to place the social human being at the center of design considerations. In 1979 Christopher Alexander published *The Timeless Way of Building* as the third leg of what might be seen as a concerted attack on the constructs of late modernism. In this book Alexander takes issue with the modern movement's

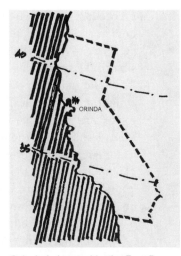

Orinda is located in the East Bay near San Francisco.

vision of itself as a break with the historical continuity of architecture. Alexander contended that the roots of architectural vocabulary were to be found in the places that people made for themselves rather than in the abstract language of science or in the romance with the machine and mechanical metaphors that so dominated later modern movement thought.

These attacks on orthodox modern movement tenets were mirrored by the work of a number of architects who were to take issue with the formal language of this period of architecture in their own work. Though these architects would not abandon the tenets of modernism altogether, they would redirect their energies to different ends. Chief among this group was Louis Kahn, who legitimized classicism as an overt modern design strategy. Kahn sensed the transcendent roots of architecture in his description of the institutions that it served and in his rejection of the absolute power of the avant-garde that the majority of modern movement architects were so taken with.

The design of the Orinda house reflects each of these criticisms. The house is the result of a knowledgeable, often witty, and sometimes profound assembly of images derived from architectural theory and history. Venturi would applaud its intellectually dexterous and insightful manipulation of the ideas that he claimed have always grounded a rigorously self-conscious architecture. The house's preoccupation with making an occasion of the otherwise mundane human activities of talking to one another and bathing give tangible evidence to Van Eyke's contentions. A keen interest in the expression of the vernacular might not satisfy Christopher Alexander, but he would maintain a similar stance concerning the importance of common architectural elements. And finally, the building's search for origins would parallel if not imitate those of architects such as Louis Kahn. This little house has come to occupy a place in thought in American architecture that far outweighs its physical size or complexity as a design that manifests historic architectural quotations, knowledge of architectural theory, a keen sense of irony, and the unabashed eclecticism that was to characterize postmodern development over the succeeding twenty-five years.

A characteristic concern for both preservation of the natural world and the way in which people experience that world provides a rich source of ideas in Moore's early architecture but disappears in his later work. This early work suggests that architectural design should be propelled both by past human experience as corporate and personal memory and by a renewed interest in the place of sensation as the generator of architectural schemes. Both of these issues are examined at length by Moore in *The Place of Houses,* written with Gerald Allen and Donlyn Lyndon in 1976, and in *Body, Memory, and Architecture,* written with Kent Bloomer in 1977. These books examine architectural design less as the outcome of the values of any particular historical or intellectual era than from a point of view about how architecture is experienced. This kind of experience-centered architectural intelligence connects people with the natural world as well as with social traditions in these statements of design intentions. It is this emphasis on the role of human sensation as experience in conceiving architectural designs, combined with Moore's early concern for the natural world, that makes the house at Orinda such a special piece of technological architecture.

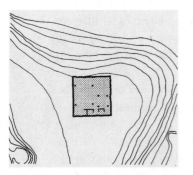

Site plan of Orinda atop a hill surrounded by valleys.

Building Description

The house is a single 28-foot square in which only the toilet is placed in a small

116

separate space. Within this square are two smaller territories that are demarcated by columns and canopies. The first and larger of the two contains an area in which to converse with friends. The second contains an oversize shower. Sleeping, cooking, and eating are granted a clearly secondary status by this plan, as they occupy the background spaces of the house. Each of these functions occupies a space that lies on a 1'9" grid that subdivides the square plan into sixteen equal increments on each side. The elevation rotates this module 90 degrees as major vertical formal organizations fall at 3'6", 7'0", 10'6", 14'0", and

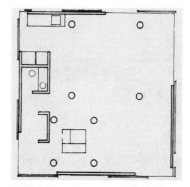

Orinda is a 28' square house based on a 1'9" square bay that also serves as a module for the development of the house's section.

17'6" increments. The house is constructed of inexpensive, commercially available building materials with the exception of the eight Tuscan columns that hold up the roof canopies, which are the legacy of a hotel fire.

The site of the house is atop a hill in the small community of Orinda, which lies east of Berkeley on the east side of the San Francisco Bay. Entry to this site is gained through a long, winding drive that removes inhabitants from the hustle and bustle of the

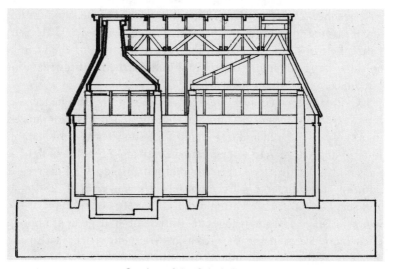

Section of the Orinda house.

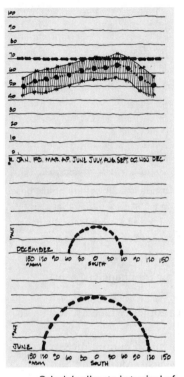

Orinda's climate is typical of northern locations near oceans.

California highway environment. At the termination of this drive lies a secluded piece of land dominated by rolling, sparsely wooded hills. The house itself was to be the first of a group of buildings that curled around the top of one of these hills. Views in all directions from the site are of a beautiful collection of northern California valleys.

CLIMATE AND SUNLIGHT

Like other Bay Area communities, Orinda experiences a climate that is very benign. High temperatures in July, August, and September average 69, 70, and 70 degrees Fahrenheit respectively. Relative humidity presents little problem, as it ranges from 59 to 86 percent during these months. Winter temperatures are again mild. Low temperatures in December, January, and February average 43, 44, and 46 degrees Fahrenheit respectively. Winter months are characterized by frequent, if not heavy, rainfall. Extreme minimum temperatures have reached 25 degrees Fahrenheit in December. The summers are dry. Extreme maximum temperatures have reached 103 degrees Fahrenheit in June. In general, the climate context of the Orinda house is what one might expect of a mid-northern-latitude city located near a major body of water.

Orinda is located at 37 degrees north latitude, and hence seasonal variations in natural luminescence are much less pronounced than those of the midland of Finland. The sun rises at 4:45 A.M. on June 21 and sets at 7:15 P.M., creating a day of 14.5 hours of light at the summer solstice. It reaches a maximum altitude of 74 degrees at noon in midsummer. On December 21, the sun rises at 7:30 A.M. and sets at 4:30 P.M., creating a day of 8 hours of sunlight at the winter solstice. The sun reaches an altitude of 30 degrees at noon in midwinter. Skies in the Bay Area are frequently overcast in the morning as the fog rolls inland from the ocean, but they normally clear by midmorning.

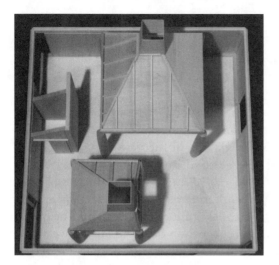

The interior of Orinda with its two canopies.

The Mechanics of Technological Form

The walls of the house are constructed of a frame system that was developed in the United States in the late nineteenth century. In this system, small-dimensioned wood is tied together by nails that were industrially manufactured in the United States after 1850. This nailed-together assembly of sticks is made rigid by adding sheathing to one or both of its surfaces. The frame plus the sheathing creates a membrane. This composite structure is much stronger than either material would be alone. The frame members of the system provide cross-sectional area to provide lateral stiffness for the assembly. The sheathing prevents slender frame members from buckling and maintains the orthogonal shape of the assembly as a whole.

The walls support the roof structure at its midpoint rather than at its corners. The 2" × 12" beam that cantilevers from this wall is testimony to the mechanics of support of the corner in that it bears only one-fourth of the weight borne by structure not at an edge or midsection. The roof is spanned by regularly spaced two-by-sixes that rest on one end on this 2" × 12" perimeter beam and at the center of the house on a 3'6" deep truss constructed of two-by-sixes. The weight brought to bear on this truss is transmitted through another

The underside of Orinda's roof.

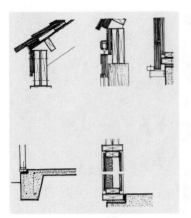

Wall section details of the Orinda house. Drawings by Andrzej Piotrowski

series of evenly spaced two-by-sixes to the Tuscan columns, which then bring this weight to the ground.

Orinda's weather envelope is minimally insulated. The 2" × 4" frame walls contain 2" of fiberglass insulation, but the floor and ceiling are not insulated. There is no glazing in the vertical openings and hence no thermal resistance in these areas. The 3/8" Plexiglas of the skylight also offers almost no resistance to the flow of heat through it in either direction. The major preoccupation of the weather envelope is thus its ability to shed moisture rather than any significant mechanical ability to provide any but the most minimal of thermal breaks with exterior temperatures. What auxiliary heat is needed in the interior of the house is provided by an electric resistance heater that is hung from the ceiling.

The two sources of natural light in the house are the large 7'0" × 21'0" skylight that frames the ridge beam and the large floor-to-ceiling openings at the corners of the house. The wall openings are unequal in size and differ in orientation, allowing much different kinds of light to enter the house. The 12'3" × 12'3" opening in the northwest corner of the house allows afternoon light into the conversation area. The 7'0" × 7'0" opening of the diagonal corner illuminates the shower with the early morning light of the southeast. The remaining two openings are 1'9" × 7'0" and do not illuminate specific areas of the house. Light from the skylight is almost always diffuse because it is reflected by the 3'6" deep walls of this opening. Sunlight from the vertical openings is reflected from the gray brown pavers of the floor. As the sun moves in the sky as a function of the time of day or the season of the year, the pattern of shadows cast by these vertical openings changes accordingly.

Analysis of Technological Form
TECHNOLOGICAL FORM AS HISTORIC CONSTRUCT

The design of the house derives from a number of formal ideas that exemplify the technological thought of other architectural eras. These ideas are not literally quoted but serve rather as a reference for the ways in which architecture has attempted to mentally as well as physically place inhabitants in a world of natural force. The forms of this historic placement are borrowed, reshaped, and knit together in the Orinda house to create a statement that, while firmly ground-ed in architectural history, proposes a renewed sense of the meaning and significance of ideas that relate building as a human act to the sense of what nature is as well as what it does in a contemporary context.

This design begins with the decision to create a single room rather than multiple rooms to accommodate the simple yet varied activities of a bachelor's domestic needs. Only the toilet is enclosed in this plan. This selection might be viewed as a reference to Lau-gier's drawing of a primitive hut, which suggests that the basis of all building is the rational modification of nature to create the basic re-quirements of human shelter. It might be seen as a reference to an eighteenth-century Japanese teahouse in a garden as a place where nature might be understood through contemplation rather than ac-tion; as a kind of Jeffersonian one-room cabin of a simpler time in American history that bound its inhabitants directly to a tangible understanding of the forces of nature; or perhaps as an appreciation of early modern American domestic architecture such as Mies van der Rohe's Farnsworth House. In each case, a human conception of people's relationship to nature drives what might be seen as the most elemental architectural statement of that proposition. Lau-gier's primitive hut is the minimal classical rearrangement of exist-ing trees in the forest to cover and mark a place of human inhabita-tion. The Japanese teahouse conforms to the Buddhist tradition of reduction to essentials. The farmhouse asserts independence from the structures of an industrial economy. The Farnsworth House cre-ates a dwelling between two planes that allows nature to flow through it. Utilitarian simplicity, formal minimalism, and primitive natural roots each anchor Orinda conceptually.

FORMAL ROOTS OF THE FRAME, ENVELOPE, AND LIGHT OPENINGS

The frame of the Orinda house refers to a varied legacy of architec-tural antecedents. The bisection of the square plan by a ridge beam that is held up by piers is shared by a long history of buildings. The columns are Tuscan, but their organization is that of a Roman shel-ter for a god. The frame of the roof and its ridge beam is akin to the organization of the roof of a Japanese *minka* (farmhouse) but is rewritten in the standardized stick forms of the industrial revolution that are found in American garage roofs. The ridge beam as a truss testifies to the industrial revolution's ability to create railroad bridges. Support at the midsection rather than at the corners of perimeter walls is reminiscent of Louis Kahn's similar preoccupation in the Richards Medical Center. The frame of Orinda consciously recalls each of these architectural junctures in a complex overlay of architectural ideas that underlie its form.

The formal antecedents of Orinda's weather envelope are as varied as those of the frame. The central notion of this house as a pavilion in the garden is anchored in English, French, and Italian landscape traditions of the seventeenth and eighteenth centuries. The roof of the house recalls Japanese thatch, and the floor is made of the cobblestones of the street or square of a medieval European village. The walls combine the modern abstraction of the dematerialization of the wall and the pragmatics of the American barn door. The absent corner is clear reference to the preoccupation of Frank Lloyd Wright with spatial containment. The materials from which the house is assembled represent the most common commercial building components, but the forms that they are assembled to take are not those of the late twentieth century but rather those of a broad intellectual history of architecture.

Again, the formal ideas that are the progenitors of the way in which sunlight is manipulated by the openings of the house are modern and classical, Eastern and Western in their origins. The oculus of the center of the house recalls the Pantheon as the classic luminescent connection of the interior of a place of dwelling with the light of the sky. While this opening tangibly connects the empirical sky with the interior as the terrestrial home of the gods, it also brings the metaphoric home of the gods as the transcendent heavens into the tangible space of human inhabitation. The luminescent corners are mindful of Frank Lloyd Wright's Freeman House near Los Angeles, in which the two corners of the living room in this textile block house become windows. The floor-to-ceiling vertical openings of the wall are akin to those of the Farnsworth House as the dematerialization of the wall.

PLAN FORM

The plan of the house is a square, 28'0" on each side. The sides of this square are subdivided into sixteen divisions of 1'9" each. The

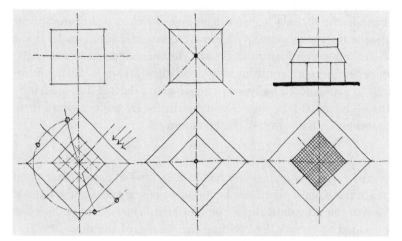

The plan form of Orinda is a rational square divided into sixteen
equal sections. The square is insensitive to the natural empirical
conditions that surround it.

resulting neutral 16 x 16 grid is the product of the rational architectural thought that was emerging in the early 1960s in works such as
Louis Kahn's Trenton Bath House. To place such a shape in nature
is to draw attention to the difference between empirical and rational
architectural thought. Gravity would certainly prefer a rectangle to
a square because it presents the opportunity to span the shorter dimension. Climate presents different problems for different sides of
the house because each orientation requires a different configuration to protect inhabitants from variations in wind, moisture, and
temperatures that prevail during different seasons of the year. And
finally, sunlight provides the least symmetrical of natural forces as it
transverses the sky from east to west and from horizon to apex and
back each day.

Placing a perfectly symmetrical plan within a context that
would seem to call for different responses to each orientation might
be viewed as an expression of indifference to the requests that differences in natural forces make on form. This view is shared by de-
terminists, who think of response to such forces as primarily a function of how a building, like a machine, performs. An alternative
view of the way in which human beings create buildings that inform
them about their place in the context of dynamic and asymmetrical
natural forces would be to note how these phenomena change by
allowing them to be seen against a regular and unchanging form.

Thus in the Orinda house the empirical forces of nature appear against the background of a rational square plan. Differences in the kinds and levels of natural light and climate that occur as a function of orientation are confronted by four identical walls. Frame members are confronted by spans of equal length. Forces that are felt by the body and can be measured empirically are paired with a form that is an ideal creation of the human mind.

THE RIDGE BEAM BISECTING THE SQUARE

Form in architecture is not excepted from laws of natural force, and hence this square plan must be modified in ways that allow natural force to be pragmatically accommodated. This accommodation is provided at Orinda by dividing the square of the plan into two equal rectangles. The center of these rectangles is marked by a ridge beam located on the center line of the house. In this way, the problem of the span of a perfectly symmetrical square floor plan is defeated in a manner that is elegant from an intellectual and from a pragmatic standpoint. The bisection of the roof plane calls out the property of line symmetry of the square without doing damage to its initial condition as point symmetry. This bisection thus both solves the pragmatic problem of spanning a square and enriches the rational geometric plan form of that square.

But to treat this ridge beam as only a clever pragmatic preserva-

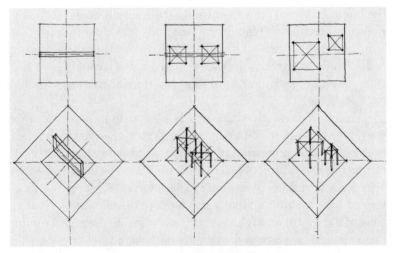

The ridge beam bisects the square and is held aloft by two canopies
that preserve the symmetry of the square.

tion of a rational premise would be to do damage to the role of human memory in creating meaning in architecture. As a cultural artifact, the ridge beam is the center of the roof that covers human habitation. It is this center that preserves the human mind and spirit, as well as the needs of the human body, and thus this unique building element has gained a special place in the collective human memory of place or, perhaps more important, of being in places. The ridge of a house not only centers its roof structure but in so doing becomes a symbol for a centered existence within that form. It is a unique place in a dwelling that has come to secure the human psyche as it gathers the live and dead loads of the roof rafters that it helps to support.

THE ROOF AND THE SKY

The roof of a building is the part of the weather envelope that shelters from temperature, sunlight, and moisture from the sky. Instead of supporting as does the floor or horizontally separating as does the wall, the roof covers. This act of covering has acquired a specific shape that might be traced to the combined need of the roof to span space and to shed moisture. The formal outcome of these mechanics has traditionally been a gabled and opaque structure.

Covering implies a kind of protection that is not given to openings. But the roof of Orinda is bisected by a giant 7'0" × 21'0" skylight that opens this surface to the sky. The boundary of the house has been violated at a place that makes inhabitants vulnerable to their exterior context. This opening powerfully reconnects inhabitants to a domain from which they are normally held separate: the sky. This reconnection is consistent with the reconnections forged by the floor and walls of the house. As the floor reconnects inhabitants with the earth and the walls with the landscape, so the void in the roof sensually reconnects inhabitants with the sky. Each of these is a realm of nature just as it is a realm of humankind. The earth supports life, the landscape is the domain of living things, and the sky is the domain of the gods who bring order to all.

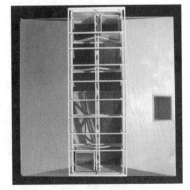

The ridge beam of Orinda bisects the skylight of the roof and is presented to inhabitants against the sky.

THE RIDGE BEAM IN THE LIGHT

The ridge beam is centered in this opening. It would normally mark the center of the opaque surface of the roof. Placing the ridge beam in a position to be viewed against the day or night sky allows this structural element to be seen against the context that makes it necessary and to which it might draw associations. The ridge beam might be seen to center the human domain as the sky centers the natural domain. In either case, human thought and activity take place not on an undifferentiated field but rather on one that has delimiting boundaries (exterior walls and the horizon) and hence has a place that might be noted as the center of a territory that has an edge. The ridge beam locates that center as being overhead as the apex of the sky vault identifies the center of the sky.

THE ROLE OF COLUMNS AT ORINDA

The ridge beam would be conventionally supported by a wall or column at each end. In the Orinda house, this single point of support is divided among four columns that, in turn, mark two special areas within the house. The two pairs of four wooden Tuscan columns each support a plywood-sheathed two-by-six-framed canopy that rises to support each end of the ridge beam. True to the eclectic tastes of postmodernism, these found objects are incorporated into the scheme of the house with wit and a modicum of irony. Each pair of columns marks an area that supports a special activity within the house. The first, a large 11'8" square, houses a place of conversation and social gathering. The second, a 7'6" square, contains the shower, a special place for cleansing the body and perhaps the spirit. Both of these conventional household activities are raised to an unconventional status by bounding them with a form normally used to specify a place of religious significance. The irony of housing what many people would consider as mundane secular activities such as talking and bathing within architectural forms of religious significance is consistent with what Moore would call a "refreshed vision of where and by extension of who we are." Space identified by these eight columns identifies human activities of special significance while the walls mark a more general space of inhabitation.

CANOPIES AND LIGHT

A small portion of the light taken in by the skylight is directed to the interior of the surface of the canopies that are supported by the columns. The undersides of the canopies are painted a reflective white in contrast to the dark stain of the roof deck. The canopies thus become a kind of natural light fixture. They reflect the light that enters them from the large skylight above in such a way as to create a place of relative brightness in the midst of shadows. This overhead illumination, in conjunction with the territorial marking of the four columns that support them, declares the spaces beneath them to be special places within the domain of the house. When electrically lit at night, they retain this sense of luminescence in contrast to the dark, light-absorbing surface of the remainder of the ceiling. In this sense, the light of these canopies remains constant while that of the sky is always changing, reversing the sense of temporal and transcendent natural light that is identified by the skylight and the vertical openings of the house.

The interior of the large canopy of light covers the conversation area of the house. Photograph courtesy of Rita B. Bottoms, Special Collections, Henry Library, University of California, Santa Cruz.

COLUMN, WALL, AND CORNER

The technological role of these columns is made clear by contrasting them with the support provided by the wall. The column represents an architectural system of support in which the space between supports is dominant. In this case, the column marks the corner of the territory that houses a human activity that is raised to ceremonial importance. The exterior edge of the roof of the Orinda house is supported by a beam that sits atop a frame-bearing wall. Each of these walls, however, is only 14 feet long, half the length of each side of the house. Each of these walls is withdrawn from the corners of the building, creating various size openings. The structural relationship between these two systems is made vivid by their juxtaposition. The columns are greatly oversized both for the space they occupy and for the structural function they fulfill. They organize the spaces within them by marking the corners with material while the sides of this territory are left open to their surroundings. At the outer edge of the house, the 14-foot frame walls support beams that cantilever over each corner. The corner is left without visible means of support. There is a structural daring to the larger northwest opening, 12'3" on a side, that has to do both with its absolute cantilever and with its size in relation to the size of the house. The opening for the shower is just as large in relation to the canopied area that it addresses. This comparison of too much material of the column contrasted with too little material at the corners of the building's outer envelope creates a heightened sensual awareness of the role of each of these structural systems as a means of ordering space. The first controls the corner with its mass, and the second abandons the control of the corner to the landscape that lies beyond the boundaries of the house.

THE CORNER AS TERRITORIAL MARKER

Barn door walls on overhead tracks allow sections of wall to cover the large openings at the corners of the house or be pulled back to rest parallel to respective opaque wall sections on each house face. The result is a house as a single space that might be totally open at

The mass of the corner column seen against the void of the envelope corner. Photograph courtesy of Rita B. Bottoms, Special Collections, Henry Library, University of California, Santa Cruz.

the corners. The corner is a fundamental identification of human territory. To enclose a corner is in many ways to initiate inhabitation. Whether a corner marks the limits of a property, the initiation of a garden, the extent of a building, or the beginning of a room, this configuration of material is among the most powerful ways that people have developed to locate what is their own domain as opposed to all other domains. To allow all four corners of a house to become void, to allow all other domains to freely invade that of the house, is a compelling commentary on the role of this element of construction in architecture. When open, the light, climate, and visual extension of the natural environment enter the Orinda house at the very place at which the exclusion of these events has traditionally stated the otherness of the human domain. The corner as void restates the direct human connection to the natural world of other living things as a powerful sensual experience in contrast to the opaque corner created by the closed barn door.

CORNERS AND SPATIAL COMMUNICATION

The lines of spatial communication set up by the columns are orthogonal. The lines of spatial communication set up by the four walls are diagonal. The columns as vestiges of rational order remain geometrically placed. The walls are shifted along the exterior surface of the house to create a series of pragmatically driven openings. The south- and west-facing walls are slid back to within one module, 1'9", of the corner, allowing the opening southwest corner of the building to be as large as possible while retaining the logic of the open corner. The two other walls remain in the center of the span, recalling the original logic of the system. The outcome is openings created by manipulating the exterior wall as a structural system that reinforces the house's orientation and interior use. The large northwest opening extends the conversation area covered by the larger of the two columned canopies to the outside. The diagonal southeast corner creates a second symmetrical opening that extends the shower to the outside. The two unsymmetrical openings to the southwest and northeast extend the remnants of the square floor plan and house the kitchen and the bed. The spatial communication created by the orthogonal columns is, conversely, terminated by opaque walls. Thus a spatial order of rational containment is superimposed on an empirical spatial order of incompleteness that must look to its context to be bounded.

THE PHENOMENAL FLOOR

The floor of the Orinda house is made of brown paver bricks that are only enough higher than the ground around them to create a surface that can shed rather than collect water. This location creates a place that is the barest of necessary modifications of the ground to create a level opening on which to reside. Because it is made of an earthen brown brick, it modifies the substance of the surrounding earth only slightly. Because it rests just slightly above the ground, it is the most minor of possible modifications of an uneven terrain. This surface may be interpreted to manifest the most primitive of human places, a clearing in the woods or prairie, or suggest the fundamental difference between what nature makes—the earth sculpted continuously by competing natural forces—and what humans make: natural material reorganized in a pattern of a flat, level square of brick pavers that is uniquely the product of the human hand and mind. In either case, the relationship that this floor at grade forges with its surroundings when the walls are pulled back and the corners of the house are left open is more that of juncture than of separation as a function both of material and of location.

TEMPORAL AND TRANSCENDENT SUNLIGHT

The differentiation by orientation of the vertical openings of the house directly contrasts with the skylight, which is always open to the sky vault above. While the northwest corner of the house allows afternoon light to flood the house from the side, the large south and east openings allow particularly the horizontal light of winter mornings to penetrate the sleeping and bathing spaces of the house. But the light that descends into the house from the skylight records the

The sunlight that enters Orinda from its side openings reflects the position of the sun and thus the time of day, whereas the light from the skylight is baffled and appears in the house as an even, timeless illumination. Model photograph by Andrzej Piotrowski.

more uniform luminescent conditions of the reflected light of the sky vault. In this sense, it connects house inhabitants directly to the heavens. It is a connection that cannot be modified or closed off, as can any of the wall openings. It uniformly addresses and directly connects inhabitants with the source of life and the tempo of time with which we measure the coming and going of our individual existence. The sky has often been represented in human myth as a place of immutability in contrast to the ever changing surface of the earth. Orinda's skylight declares this understanding by making the skylight and ridge beam partners in forging a human connection to the location of spiritual, if not physical, permanence. This modern metaphysical definition of human existence might be seen in contrast to the sliding barn doors that modify human contact with all that changes in the tangible landscape. These openings are a wonderful combination of the pragmatism of the American barn door superimposed on an intellectualization of the modern movement to create a place that oscillates in human experience between an all-inclusive existence under the canopy of a pavilion located in nature and the protection of the opaque corner. The horizontal light that enters the house through these openings brings with it the images of all that surrounds the house, from the reflections of nearby plants to the end of the house's tangible domain at the horizon.

Technological Form as Metaphoric Thought

If culture as manifest in form is episodic, leaving only a residue of original intentions in the building, each era leaves behind responses to natural force as its unchanging counterpart. The Orinda house takes every opportunity not simply to restate this context of natural force but to overstate it. The role of column, wall, and ridge beam as elements of historic form derived from pragmatic technological need is reunderstood in a manner in this house that records the process of creating cultural symbols from pragmatic technology. It represents an intellectual art of creation that attempts to reveal the complexity of the pragmatic and symbolic role played by technological elements in the space of time that it takes to enter and experience a tiny one-room house. Within this house are a series of formal references not to the images that these historical technological responses have taken but rather, through these forms, to the ideas that they propel concerning the character of the natural world and its inhabitation. These forms thus constitute a kind of architectural mythology that treats nature as the subject of its formal stories. In each of these stories lies a kernel of metaphoric knowledge that has accreted over time to become the foundation of the modern natural myth. This historical foundation might be seen to either reinforce or confront contemporary values. In either case, a firm knowledge of the history of this thought is requisite to understanding the contemporary condition.

To achieve this kind of instant insight into the role of technology in architecture requires that role to be presented in powerful sensual terms that require house inhabitants to take notice of them. Most contemporary technological responses in architecture have become so habitual, given this commentary, as to render the power of technology in buildings to place people in the world mute. The repetitive and thoughtless manipulation of these technologies in the vast majority of architecture has created a civilization unaware of the role of architecture as a mediator between the rational world of the mind and the empirical world of the body. To reawaken this dormant understanding in a less-than-sensitive era requires that these relationships be presented in sensual forms that refuse to go unnoticed. This proposal contends that the root of the return to this understanding must be sensual because it is our senses that inform our mental understanding of the outside world.

METAPHORICAL TECHNOLOGY AS SENSUALLY REVEALED BELIEF

The critical idea in each of these manipulations is not as much a matter of the selective assembly and role reversals of architectural elements as quotations of historical formal ideas, though their selection and manipulation demonstrate a level of understanding of architectural history that is rare among designers. What is truly unique about this house is the way in which it confronts inhabitants with manifestations of responses to natural force. The floor just above grade and the barn door openness of the corners allow this ground and the climate to flow into and through the house. Inhabitants are directly touched by the natural context. The traditional place of the envelope of the house as the element that separates the interior domain from its exterior circumstances, thus creating the need for the entry as a special kind of architectural connection, is blurred if not done away with altogether in this design. Sunlight that would normally enter the house through traditional windows now floods the skylight framing the ridge beam above and streaks through the absence of building envelope at different corners of the house, registering the time of day or the timelessness of the sky. Finally, the role reversal of the ridge beam rewritten as a truss, suspended in the gaping hole of the skylight, is mirrored in the overscaled support provided by the Tuscan columns as compared with the seemingly underscaled support of the roof at its corners. These often clever reorganizations of architectural technology serve to present the natural forces that each responds to in an unconventional manner. This flouting of technological convention is not superficial or purposeless. Each of these modifications essentially points out natural forces in a way that allows them to be seen in a new light and thus appreciated in a way that has been dulled by convention. The skylight and ridge beam unite the interior of the house with the heavens in a way that reminds inhabitants anew of the role that the heavens have played in people's sense of belonging to a larger pattern that rules the universe. The light canopies below this skylight create a reverse hearth in which light streams into the special place below. Natural light enters the corners of the house, telling the time of day and season of the year to inhabitants. Light reflected by the landscape beyond the corners of the house is essential to the definition of completion within the continuity of domains. Form powerfully connects the interior of this house with the physical and mental cosmos that provides its context. Each sensual confrontation is linked to the history of thought with which human beings have defined their place in nature by referencing historic building conditions that have encoded this thought. The duty of dwelling as technology is thus seen to be less about what works than about the common set of values that technological form proposes.

This kind of manipulation of technological form might be termed *sensually revealed belief*. Its first task is to place the inhabitant of the house powerfully in nature as the context of a hypersensed natural domain. The site in this context is meant to be not only the visible landscape but also the sun, sky, weather, and gravity. Design elements that normally place inhabitants in relation to the natural world are each reconsidered and remolded in turn to create conditions in which the house inhabitants become unusually sensually aware of their existence and place in the ensemble of the building as a vehicle for locating people among these felt characteristics of the natural domain. What is important about each of these representations is not only that they stir greater sensual awareness than would conventional manipulations of technology in a house but that this heightened sensual awareness connects to a set of larger ideas concerning the role of architecture in placing people in their natural surroundings. The roof skylight not only allows the interior of the house to be illuminated from above but, by framing the ridge beam in the lightness of the heavens, suggests that we are always spiritually as well as physically covered by this architectural element. The floor of dark brown paver bricks just above grade reminds us that the first dwelling was a simple flattened clearing in nature. To make that clearing level is a uniquely human act. The screenless, glassless, full-height openings at the corners of the house make the dematerialized wall of the modern movement into a sensual reference to the Garden of Eden rather than an intellectual abstraction. The roof-covered floor is mindful of the most minimal environmental protection, one that shields inhabitants from sun and moisture but otherwise allows the earth and the air to touch inhabitants inside the house, just as they might in a state less mediated by machines. As the barn door corners are closed, the horizontal connection to the exterior is severed, and the vertical connection of the earth to heavens proposed both by the outer envelope roof as a canopy and by the two smaller interior canopies becomes spatially dominant. The openings at the apex of each canopy ensure that the light sky or the night sky will enter each as the interior space under each flows into the heavens.

Here, then, is a tiny house that weaves historical and personal values together within a context of becoming sensually aware of the natural world as a powerful setting for human existence. Each of the formal proposals of this house asks inhabitants to rethink the character of their original place in nature as complement and contrast to their place in the natural world today. Machines can modify each of these natural forces but do so at a cost of tangible distance and mental abstraction. People are no longer able to connect beliefs directly with a context that they are able to feel. The reconnection of sense with belief through the manipulation of technological form in architecture allows the human body again to become the progenitor of the stories that give value to nature.

7. Wall House

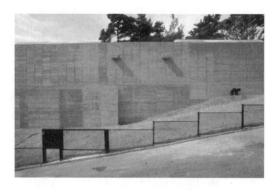

Background

The Wall House is one of the early works of Tadao Ando. Like so many of his contemporaries, Ando sought to find his initial architectural voice first in the design of private houses. Houses are often relatively small projects that lack the kind of programmatic complexities and constraints that characterize larger projects and hence tend to promote the enunciation of ideas that are of interest to the architect as a designer. The Wall House is a case in point.

Botond Bognar calls Ando an "architect of resistance." The resistance that Bognar refers to is to the material values that accompanied the American occupation of Japan after World War II. There is a depth to the need for this "resistance" that might not be apparent to an initial understanding of what needs to be resisted by a house and why this resistance is so necessary to human well-being.

Japanese culture is rooted both in the beliefs of the native Jamon and Yayoy tribes that first settled the islands and in successive Buddhist invasions in the sixth, twelfth, and seventeenth centuries. The

The Wall House is located near Osaka, Japan.

Jamon were the first to come. They were the hunter-gathers of Japanese culture who crossed land bridges twelve thousand years ago to reach these islands from mainland Asia. The Jamon appeasement of nature took the form of rites that honored the powers of the natural world as equivalent to those of humankind. These rituals were codified later in the animism of Shinto beliefs. In this system of thought, all animals, plants, trees, rocks, and even the earth itself are endowed with the same spirit that inhabits humankind. The world is not bifurcated into the province of humans and the province of nature or even into the province of animate versus inanimate objects. It exists as one common field of spiritual energy that provides the motive force for being, a character in life, and a reason to respect the death of all things. The Yayoy came to these islands eight thousand years later and brought with them the more permanent and sophisticated traditions of farmers. Nature was not the enemy to these people but the source of all sustenance. The artwork that they left behind was not that of the utilitarian water jug decorated with rope-like figures of the Jamon but miniature clay granaries that spoke of their ties to the land.

The invasion of Buddhism, first in the sixth and then later in the twelfth and seventeenth centuries, from continental Asia brought with it the contemplative tradition that is the ground of many Eastern philosophies. Jacob Bronowski has said that the fundamental difference between the East and the West is that the West learns by taking action on the world while the East learns by contemplating the qualities of that world. This is not just a difference between the empiricism of Western science and the mysticism of the East but more fundamentally a definition of the two ways in which human beings come to know themselves and the world they live in. Action sees knowledge in the outer world. Human beings come to know that world, and by extension themselves, through the manipulation of that world. Contemplation sees knowledge as an extension of an understanding of the self. The knowledge of contemplation mistrusts the appearance of the outer world. Just as human beings have essences that are not apparent in their tactile form, so do all other things. In the Eastern thought of Buddhism, all that exists is but a manifestation of a single force. The role of thought is to pierce the veil of superficial reality in search of this singular source that underlies the superficial world of things that house human existence.

The Buddhism that Sen no Ryko brought to Japan at the beginning of the seventeenth century was housed in the contemplation of the tea ceremony. His interpretation of this Buddhist act of sharing a drink of tea from a common bowl at the end of meditation was to reduce the ceremony to a few simple acts so that each might be contemplated in search of the essence of being. The preparations for this ceremony are elaborate but yield simple outcomes. The charcoal to heat the tea is made by the tea master in a beautiful shape and then washed. All of this effort and beauty will be consumed as the charcoal burns to heat the tea water. The floor of the vessel that the charcoal is to be burned in is covered with sand to protect it and the floor below from the heat of the charcoal fire. This sand is raked into a beautiful miniature landscape by the tea master and will also be consumed by the burning charcoal. The tea water and tea leaves are carefully chosen for their unique qualities. The water is heated and the tea leaves are placed in it in strict accordance with the rules that govern the performance of the ceremony. The behavior of guests is likewise a matter of strict adherence to a ritualized code of conduct. Only commentary that is directly focused on the ceremony is allowed. Conversation concerning the mundane issues of everyday life in the world outside of the ceremony is forbidden. The tea ceremony and the teahouse that is created to give a place for this ritual are thus a kind of mental cleansing. They eliminate the confusion and attendant superficiality of everyday life so that the essence of a single act might be contemplated in depth. Reality is revealed not in the variety of matter and energy of the apparent world but in a simplicity of form that has been stripped to its essential core so that its essence might emerge for human contemplation. All is one. Oneness is difficult to grasp because it is clouded by the profusion of appearances brought to the mind by human senses.

This cultural heritage of contemplating the essence of things as their oneness is at stake in the word "resistance." The occupation of Japan by the West brought with it the values of materialism. These values were to become the second culture of Japan. Against the background of Shinto as all things being endowed with spirit and that of Buddhism as the knowledge of the essence of things through their contemplation was overlaid the powerful Western constructs of modern science, Western technology, modes of production, capitalism, consumerism, and democracy. The result was the kind of urban Japanese culture that is manifest most clearly in large industrial cities such as Tokyo and Osaka. The virtues of traditional Japanese society might be honored in form under these new conditions, but their meaning was quickly being dissipated in the Western rush to produce and acquire goods. Tadao Ando, like Sen no Ryko three hundred years before, seeks to refocus the Japanese mind on the richness of its traditional way of knowing.

A seminal myth differentiates the ways in which Eastern and Western cultures have come to see nature and the place of human beings in this context. In Christian mythology, humankind is cast from the Garden of Eden for acquiring the knowledge of self-awareness. The transgression and its result were the same. By becoming aware of the difference between humans and nature, the human mind forged an irreversible difference between the two. People were forever cast out of nature. They were directed by Christian mythology to go out and "subdue" the other living things of the earth. Nature was henceforth to become the other, what José Ortega y Gasset would refer to as the source of "difficulties and facilities" (297). The difficulties Gasset describes represent the difference between human and natural needs. The difficulties are the product of the human desire not only for material well-being but for spiritual well-being in that every life constitutes the project of becoming that which a human being desires to be within a natural context that has its own agenda. Nature's facilities, according to Gasset, are found through technology. They constitute the human ability to construct a supranature to fulfill its desires. The world of nature provides the unspiritualized ground for the human spiritual search for what it desires to become. The quest is not for the return to the garden but for its manipulation through technology to serve human desire.

How different must be a world that has not been cleaved in two by Christian mythology. In the oneness of the spirit of animism and the unity of origin of Buddhism lies the counterpoint of the Christian construct of the division of humans from nature. What has not been divided need not be reunited. The desires of humans are reflections of the desires of nature. To understand one is not to manipulate it from without but to recognize these convergences from within. The Eastern bridge does not describe the differences between the water and the land by crossing the water. It does not point out the separation of the two banks of the river by connecting them. It does not suggest the prowess of human technological skill by spanning great chasms with a single arch. It brings the human being to the

The garden and teahouse of Katsura Imperial Palace.

river so that the river might be understood as a member of the world. It mingles the land with the water, clouding the distinction between the two. It makes of the person, the water, and the land a oneness rather than a twoness or a threeness. It is small and simple and infinitely complex in what it suggests about human relationships to the natural world. Its meaning is found not in how it performs but in the understanding that it perennially brings to the river and stones that are being crossed.

The East has always served as a mirror for Western thought. As in Bronowski's comparison, the West requires an external measure to fully understand its own character. The West sets primary value on an empirical world. Truth lies in statements that can be demonstrated as measurable outcome. The East sees material to be only a mask of the inner reality of things and their significance to human existence. The essence of these things can only be arrived at through contemplation of ideas that cannot be seen or felt. Comparing these two points of view does not simply identify their differences but allows each culture to see its activities anew. In this new vision, the opportunity for revised thought that more aptly or more fully reflects the human condition arises. Eastern architectural thought opens technology to the contemplative understanding of what it, in essence, is rather that the knowledge of what it does.

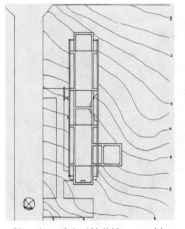

Site plan of the Wall House with a street on the city side of the house and a forest on the opposite side.

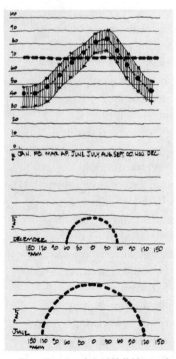

The climate of the Wall House is tempered by its island location.

Description of the Building

The Wall House was designed in 1976 and constructed in 1977 in the prefecture of Hyōgo near the city of Osaka. The house is located on the outskirts of the city between a residential street and a national forest. The Wall House is a lineal two-story structure divided into two parts by an exterior court located at its center. North of the court lies the portion of the house that contains the mechanical room and the kitchen on the first floor, with the tatami room and the living room above. To the south of the open court is a studio on the first floor with the two bedrooms of the house above. The bedrooms are connected to the living areas of the house by a small bridge that extends along an edge of the central courtyard.

CLIMATE AND SUNLIGHT

The climate of this area is influenced by a warm ocean current from the south, the Kuroshio, and by a cold current from the north, the Oyashio. The mountain ranges of Japan create a wide variety of microclimates within this basic framework. Winter temperatures in Hyōgo prefecture range from average lows in January of 32°F to highs of 47°F. The median temperature in January is 41°F. In July high temperatures average 87°F and lows 73°F. The median temperature in July is 81°F. Spring and fall are characterized by moderate temperatures that range from 55 to 73°F. The median temperature in March is 67°F and in September is 76°F. The relative humidity remains fairly constant throughout the year at approximately 57 percent. Moisture falls as rain, accumulating to

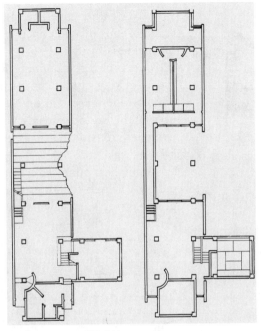

Wall House plans.

59" to 79" throughout the year with an occasional snowfall in the winter.

At 39 degrees north latitude, the sun rises at 58 degrees east of south on December 21 and sets at 58 degrees west of south. On June 21 the sun rises at 118 degrees east of south and sets at 118 degrees west of south. On noon of December 21, the sun reaches an altitude of 31 degrees. On noon of June 21 it reaches an altitude of 76 degrees. There are eight hours of sunlight per day in December and fourteen hours of sunlight in June at this latitude.

The Mechanics of Technological Form

The columns and beams that form the frame of the Wall House are constructed of poured-in-place reinforced concrete. The columns are 17¾" square in section. The beams are 19¾" deep and vary from 13¾" to 17¾" in width. Columns are spaced at 15'0" intervals and form a monolithic frame with the system of beams. The ceiling-roof that covers the living and bedroom portions of the house is a precast reinforced concrete vault 7⅜" thick. Other ceiling-roof spanning structures are flat reinforced concrete slabs 4¾" thick.

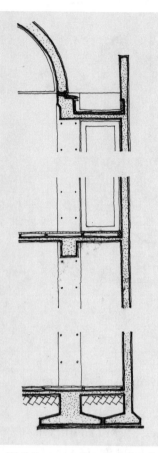

Wall House section. Drawing by Andrzej Piotrowski.

The weather envelope of the house is made of uninsulated concrete that varies in thickness from 4¾" to 7¾" and hence provides minimal insulation (R-4) against the relatively cold temperatures of the winter. Floors are also uninsulated, connecting this surface directly with the thermal conditions of the earth. All openings are single glazed.

Sunlight is admitted to the house primarily through openings that are made possible by the absence of walls. At the perimeter of the building, these openings occur only between the frame and the wall or the frame and the vault above. In the interior courtyard, the interstices of the frame are also fully glazed. The kitchen and the tatami room both have horizontal windows that extend from frame element to frame element, but not from floor to ceiling. The orientation of the house is generally along a northwest to southeast axis. Major glazing areas of the central courtyard face the southeast and the northwest.

Analysis of the Technological Form

THE WALL AS SEPARATION

The technological form of the Wall House is initiated by the placement of two very large concrete walls parallel to each other. These walls signify, just as the wall around Katsura Palace nearly three hundred years before, withdrawal from the secular world of material goods and political power into a realm of solitude and contemplation. The essence of the wall is thus never simply to separate an interior climate from the climatic stresses of the exterior but, by extension, to separate human existence from all the stresses of the outside world. The sheer, unpenetrated walls of the Wall House cleave through the sky, air, and earth to create the fundamental vertical separation that defines the initiation of a space to dwell that is separated from its broader context, be it cultural or climatic.

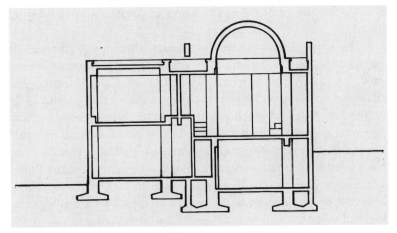

Wall House section.

Each of these walls is continuous and unpunctured. Each marks the possibility of the occurrence of different events on its two sides. The horizontal continuity of the wall is manifest in the horizontal texture of the poured concrete that is the residue of the horizontal board form-work into which it was poured. The space left between the two walls signals in its scale the difference between the inside and outside, as they are just far enough apart to suggest the definition of the sides of a room. The planelike thinness and uniform thickness of these walls suggest formal abstraction of *that*

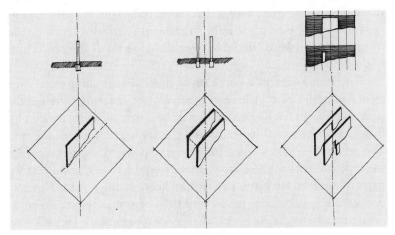

The design of the Wall House is initiated by two parallel vertical slabs that cut through the air and the earth.

which separates rather than the palpable construction of piled-up pieces.

This shape cleaves the air and the earth that it passes through. It extends up into the sky and does not rest on a foundation on the earth but rather plunges into it. There is a sense in this form of the character of not just this wall but the essence of every wall. These two structures stand independent of all else as the primordial and perennial markers of human space. They divide the world into two seminal domains: the unique province of human beings and the place in which human beings will mingle with all other living things and their processes. The lack of openings in these walls forcefully states the first obligation of the wall to divide, to separate, to allow the distinctly human notion of separation from nature to arise.

The heart of the wall is its ability to separate, so that the reconnection of domains that have been created by this separation becomes an act of human discretion. Every wall is in its essence this division that contains the possibility of connection. It is this act that first places human existence mentally as well as physically in the world.

THE FRAME AS RATIONAL, NONHIERARCHICAL ORDER

Within these two walls is a structure comprising a series of orthogonal columns and beams of approximately the same square section to form a repetitive three-dimensional grid. This grid is the rhythmic repetition prescribed by a uniform gravitational field. It is akin to the partitioning of territory by the columns in the traditional Japanese farmhouse as a nonhierarchical spatial order. It is the metaphorical order of the inner world that requires the protection of the wall.

The frame creates a corridor of space that is subdivided into eight squares in plan. The central corridor of space that these eight squares create is flanked on either side by a narrow space created by the distance between the frame and the wall. The outer of the two bays of this corridor are dedicated to rooms with uses that separate the interior of the house from outside contact. The middle three pairs of squares are given over to the heart of the house. The first pair contains the studio below and the bedrooms above; the middle pair contains the courtyard that is open to outdoor climatic and solar conditions of the sky; and the third pair contains the living area of the house.

Wall House model section.

This square grid of beams and columns is finished as a smooth rather than rough texture in contrast to the walls that enclose it. Though there are minor variations in the size of the beams overhead, the sense of the frame is one of uniformity. Columns are not differentiated in section by the amount of load that they carry, and beams assume a section that is little different than that of the columns that support them. All are much larger than they need be to serve a functional purpose. Like the wall, the frame stands as an independent gesture. Its fundamental task is to bring order to the space that has been enclosed by the two exterior walls.

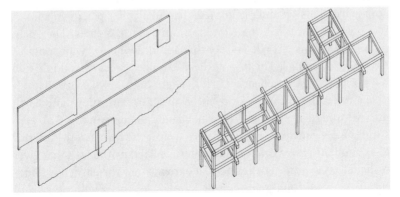

The walls and frame of the Wall House.

It may be filled with the functions of living as need dictates. The only way in which the position of these activities might be differentiated is in terms of their relationship to the garden. This is a different place in the frame because it is the juncture with the order of the world that it is not. The frame, unlike the wall, does not capture territory with its sidedness and continuity. Once captured, however, it is the frame that creates the seminal conceptual order of domain within that territory.

The light that comes between the frame and the wall names each as its essential character as they reside adjacent to each other. Sunlight enters these vertical slits perpendicular to the walls and slides along it, dissipating in intensity the farther it gets from the opening. It remains unbroken as it reflects the horizontal striations of the wall that it illuminates. Its diminution signals the interiorization that is created by the wall. Its continuity is the continuity of the wall. The column, conversely, is a discrete object. When light strikes it, each of its surfaces is illuminated to a different degree. Its shape and the open space that emerges from this shape are named by the light. It too is nearer or farther from the outside as this light diminishes. The discretely lit column adjacent to the continuously lit wall calls forth their elemental architectural functions. The frame orders and connects space; the wall encloses.

RECIPROCAL OPENINGS IN THE WALL

The northeast, city-facing wall of the house is punctured in only one place. This is a small opening, the size of a human being, into the courtyard. This opening is immediately healed by placing a similar section of wall a few feet beyond the entry that it creates. The opening in the wall is closed. The southwest, forest-facing wall contains two large openings. The first of these extends across the middle two bays of the frame and nearly the full height of this two-story space. It opens to let the natural world of the sun, air, rain, snow, and earth into the middle of the dwelling. The second opening in this wall constitutes a reciprocal action. It opens to allow the frame of the interior to expand into the world of nature unprotected by the wall that gives it shelter elsewhere. The frame that extends into the garden is mindful of the traditional teahouse of Katsura Palace. The functions of this space as the kitchen and tatami room support this analogy.

THE COURTYARD AND THE ESSENCE OF THE NATURAL WORLD

The court at the center of the house captures the garden of the outside just as the openings of a traditional Japanese house capture the garden by framing it in an opening. This space is, in a sense, the *tokonoma*, or sacred niche, of a traditional Japanese dwelling. Instead of a landscape scroll hanging on the wall of this honorific niche, the courtyard, like the garden, becomes the means to grasp the things of nature directly. As in the landscape painting, the essence of nature is captured not in the empirical realities of natural processes but in their representation. Nature in its own domain is not available to the human mind for contemplation because it has not been framed so that a limited portion of this world might be considered in depth. The courtyard divorces a piece of the natural world from its natural context so that it might become an object of contemplation. It is not in the ground at large but in the simple gesture of the earth eroding the edge of the stairs of the courtyard that the landscape might be known. It is not in the sky but in a temporal reflection on a wall that the sun might be known. It is not in a storm but in a single drop of rain captured by the courtyard that the renewal of water might be known. The courtyard houses nature as the dwelling houses its inhabitants. The room of nature is honorifically placed at the center of the house because it initiates life. It becomes

Model of the land penetrating the wall and the frame at the
center of the Wall House.

one of a triad of places that constitute dwelling. There is first the space that is within the walls and hence separated from direct contact with the world beyond. Second is the domain of dwelling that is the place where the frame is unsheathed directly in the natural world. It is fundamentally an invasion of nature by the dwelling. And finally there is the domain in which nature is captured by the confines of the house.

CAPTURING NATURE AT THE CENTER OF THE HOUSE

Wall House courtyard. Photograph courtesy of Tadao Ando.

Land, air, and sky meet in the courtyard of the Wall House. Photograph courtesy of Tadao Ando.

The courtyard is not the unbounded world of nature. It is the place where a tiny slice of the natural world is invited into the domain of the house so that it might be experienced, felt, thought of, and remembered as the focus of human attention. As in the tea ceremony, the house becomes the tea master that creates the setting to understand the beauty, meaning, and transience of nature as that of human existence itself.

At the center of the house, where the living room, studio, and bedrooms meet the courtyard, the interstices of the frame are fully glazed in opposition to the ends of the frame, where they are filled by opaque concrete panels. The living spaces are turned to face the courtyard through the vehicle of this transparency and away from the outside world. The courtyard is open to the sky and to the forest to the southeast because of the large openings that have been created in the envelope. The frame marches through this space, organizing nature in the same way that it organizes the interior of the habitational house. The nature that is invited into the house through the courtyard has been framed by the openings of the envelope and ordered by the frame that runs through it. As in the Moon Watching Pavilion of Katsura Palace, the Moon is understood not by directly observing it but by watching its reflection in a pond.

The courtyard states its symbolic mission without equivocation. Its progenitor, the courtyard of the Chinese house, might be thought of as a clever way to bring sunlight and ventilation to dense residential development in which houses shared common walls as their property lines. The functional need for these outdoor spaces is clear in these settings. But even this humble, utilitarian courtyard was not without its symbolic significance. In Feng Shui it became the connection of heaven and earth, the place where the larger world of spirit met the smaller world of the domain. Its walls framed the earth and the sky just as those of the Wall House do. The sun, air, clouds, rain, snow, and earth became the center of the house as another member of the force from which all that is springs. It is interesting that in Chinese culture, Feng Shui is not only applied to the siting and organization of a house that is to come into harmony with nature but also used to diagnose disease and to bring the human body back into a state of harmony. The

Model of the central courtyard of the Wall House from above.

meridians and pressure points of acupuncture map out the same conceptual system as does Feng Shui. There exists in this mode of thought no difference between the animate and inanimate world, between humans and nature, between the mechanics of the house and the house as a source of well-being. All is one. The garden has never been left. Its memory is simply clouded by the human mind's capacity to mistake superficial form for substance. The center courtyard of the Wall House frames and captures the simple ingredients of the natural world to benefit the human mind. The little rectangular patch of sky is seen for what it is, the perpetually changing source of life for the world. The air is felt for what it is, the manifestation of the flow of energy that is at the heart of all being. The earth is felt for what it is, the ground on which all existence takes place. It is in the particular that the universal might be captured. It is in the tactile experience that the mind might be focused. It is in the uncovering of the essence that the truth might be sought.

THE FLOOR AND THE EARTH

The floor of the Wall House might easily be overlooked among its more aggressively stated companions, but it should not be. This is really not a two-story house in the conventional sense of that term. It is really a single-story house that follows the land with a bridge to bedrooms that float above. The floor of the living portions of the house turns from the oak of the living room to the clay tile of the courtyard steps and the studio floor. As it passes through the courtyard, it steps down as the terrain did before the house arrived. It is formed by the earth that preceded it, not by the needs of the household. It mingles with the vegetation of the earth at its edge, making uncertain the boundary between territory that is organized by nature and territory that is organized by humans. It is in some ways the simple remaking of the earth as flat tiles that reorganize its form to accept human occupation. The floor of the studio is that occupation.

The floor of the second-story bridge and bedrooms references the floor on the earth by contrasting it with the conception of a bridge as a floor in the sky. Its genesis is no longer that of the land

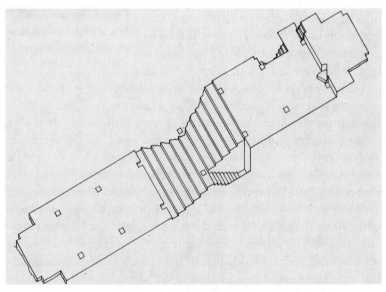

An axnometric drawing of the floor of the Wall House.

but that of the construction that occurs above the land. The little horizontal slit of sunlight that runs along the floor of the bridge to the bedrooms marks this difference. The bridge belongs to the sky and not solely to the earth. It transverses the earth not as a path on the ground but as a passage through the sky. The sun is the manifestation of the sky on the earth. The light it brings connects the heavens and the earth. It is this light that picks out the bridge as not being the progeny of the earth in the Wall House.

THE VAULT AND THE SKY

The two vaults of the house cover the human domain as the sky covers the earth. Like the walls, the roof is a part of the building envelope that separates, but again like the walls, this act of separation allows the possibility of connection. The connection that is made by these two vaults is one of thought that attends image. The sky is rarely pictured in the myths of humankind as an object that rests simply above the earth. It extends high overhead but also attaches itself to the earth and the air at the horizon. The path of the sun across this surface is clearly not rectangular. Thus the form of the heavens is normally seen as a surface that wraps around the earth in an arc. This is the shape that most readily accounts for the human perception of the sky. Contemporary culture continues this tradition by referring to light that comes from the sky as coming from the sky vault. In this vault is embedded the notion of "to be covered." A flat surface may extend indefinitely without ever protecting an inhabitant at its edges. To be covered is to have something that wraps around human beings. An embrace with another person wraps around them; clothing wraps around them, blankets wrap around them, and the heat of an open fire wraps around them. The vault of the house covers inhabitants as blankets cover their bed as the sky covers the earth.

Technological Form as Metaphorical Thought

Each of the primary technological forms of the house is named and explored individually in this design. The wall separates and in so doing provides the possibility for selective reconnection with the landscape. The frame orders the territory within as a regular spatial pattern. The floor supports human activity and in so doing references the earth, which is the ground of all human activity. The vault of the roof protects inhabitants from the sky but reconnects the dwelling to the vault of the heavens in its shape. Light names all things in and of themselves and relates them in their singleness one to the other to create a domain of things for human habitation. Human and natural existence meet and are captured by each other at the center of the house in the open courtyard as a reminder of the oneness of all existence.

Beneath this ability of technological elements to generate meaningful abstractions lies the idea that, in their essence, they have always done so. The first piling up of earth or stones contained the essential conception of separation. The first crude attempts to provide a roof with twigs and leaves contained the essential conception of "to cover." The first clearing in the woods contained the essential demarcation of a surface of human action. The first attempt to put tree branches together in a way that would allow space to be carved out of gravity contained the essential conception of order. Each of these technological building elements has changed its superficial form over the course of human history, but the essence of its form is contained in the genetic memory of the first relationship that it struck between the human mind and nature. This may have been a relationship initiated by material need, but in the action that was taken to meet that need was always the power of that act to identify the essence of the natural forces inhabited by humankind. People come to know nature through what they build, but in this act, they necessarily come to know themselves. To demarcate, to separate, to cover, and to order are not qualities of nature. They are ideas that are born of a human consciousness that inhabits nature. They are created in the act of constructing a dwelling. They become what nature is because they are what human beings are. They name the natural world as the symbolic essences of human existence. The memory of this essence is always present in the essential character of the buildings that human beings make because it was present in the origin of the act of creating this entity. The essence of origin may be masked by the attention that designers give to other issues, but it never disappears altogether. It is always sensed as the genetic memory of how that building element originally connected human beings to their natural context. The validation of this assumption lies in the ability of all peoples to enter the domain of others, no matter what their culture or era, and recognize not only the form of their dwelling but its symbolic significance. Often, the more basic the dwelling, the stronger this feeling of a sense of origins becomes. Perhaps that is because in these more primitive abodes, the same genetic memory of the role of these elements in placing human beings in their natural context is recalled with a clarity that the Wall House attempts to restate in modern terms.

Stating these elements as geometric forms is a way of universalizing them. Reducing the wall to a plane, the frame to a three-dimensional grid of squares, the roof to a semicircle, and windows to the spaces created by the area between these elements is a way of naming them as not just the particular wall, roof, floor, frame, and window in question but the underlying form of all walls, roofs, floors, frames, and windows. The wall is always a vertical partition of space that cleaves the air. The roof is always, at its heart, a surface that arcs to cover. The floor is always the flattened place in an uneven terrain, the frame is always the order of gravity, and the window is always the absence of the wall that reconnects the inner world of the dwelling with the outer world of nature. These are seen in the Wall House not as primitive gestures but as universal truths. If the Wall House restates these fundamental truths about how human beings inhabit nature, then this universality needs to find a formal voice in the universal terms of geometry. To be sure, these elements are modified to reflect the particulars of this house and its specific context, but the statement of its technological form makes just as clear the idea that this particularity is built on a set of values that have always been everywhere that people have constructed shelters.

Technological Form as Embedded Origins
This kind of technological metaphor might be called *embedded origins*. Embedded origins as metaphorical technology depend on three assumptions. The first is that a metaphorical understanding of the world is inherent in any act of making something. In this form of thought there can be no separation of the physical act of modifying the natural world and of mentally taking possession of it in a particular way. The process of taking action on the world always gives rise to a mental construct of that world that becomes embedded in the form that is created. This mental construct will remain the essential character of this creation each time that it is reproduced independent of culture or time. It is thus the embedded essence of the

first act of creation of a technological building element that is being recovered in its numerous specific manifestations, no matter what their particular form or circumstance.

This meaning arose in the first place because each of these technological forms placed people in the natural world in a specific way. Walls always separated, floors always related people to the ground, roofs always covered, frames always ordered, and windows always connected people to their surroundings. The mechanics of these forms are simply the means to place people in the natural world. They cannot be ends in themselves because foot pounds, British thermal units, and lumens have no power in and of themselves to locate people. Location in this form of thought is the recovery of technological form's original ability to create the abstractions of architecture that characterize place.

The goal of this kind of metaphor is to attempt to reveal the character of this embedded origin. Because it depended on a nonverbal form of thought in the first place, this recovery cannot be the outcome of the analysis of existing technological form. It must be perennially sought in the context of succeeding generations. Its meaning for architects lies in its revelation in the buildings that they make. The power of these technological metaphors is the power to uncover, reveal, capture, and restate the invisible essence of modifying natural force to accommodate human inhabitation.

8. Villa Savoye

Background

Villa Savoye was designed by Le Corbusier from 1929 to 1931 and was constructed in Poissy, France, as a vacation house in 1933. It is among the best-known houses of the modern movement because it completed a series of structures that Le Corbusier designed in the 1920s that manifest his famous Five Points of Architecture.

Villa Savoye was conceived of in an era of great confidence in human intellectual prowess. Major scientific discoveries in the second half of the nineteenth century and the first portion of the twentieth century had the appearance of unveiling the underlying structure of the natural world. Darwin had unmasked the mystery of the existence of the great varieties of animal life, including that of human beings, in his *On the Origin of Species,* first published in 1859. Freud had given a structure to the human mind in his conception of peoples' mental constructs as being the result of the subconscious, the ego, the superego, and the id in a series of works at the turn of the century. But as large as these discoveries were, they were overshadowed by the work of the physicists of the day. This group of Europeans put together a revolutionary and powerful concept that proposed that all matter was made up of infinitesimal and

Poissy is located near Paris, France.

indivisible particles called electrons, protons, and neutrons. J. J. Thomson discovered the electron in 1897. Ernest Rutherford named the proton in 1914. James Chadwick discovered the neutron in 1931. In 1913 Niels Bohr led a group of scientists who gave structure to the whole as electrons vibrating at specified energy levels around a nucleus of much heavier protons and neutrons called an atom, bringing to fruition a Greek theory of the structure of matter that had been posited 2,400 years before. Within this construct, all matter could be demonstrated to comprise different combinations of these electrons, protons, and neutrons as they created the elements of the atomic chart. The physical world behaved as if this chart were correct, for the most part. The human mind had finally triumphed over the secrets of nature in a way that not only reflected the behavior of the physical world but explained the underlying structure of that world. Science was no longer simply the chronicler of effects. It was now the powerful lens onto the heart of the existence of all substances that made up the world of matter and energy that surrounds human beings. The locus of human life was understood no longer in metaphysical terms such as "the nature of the good" or in religious terms such as "the will of God" but in the contemporary terms of the substructure of matter and energy.

The influence that physics in general and noted physicists such as Rutherford, Bohr, Planck, and Einstein in particular had on this and on current culture would be difficult to overestimate. This brand of physics produced a highly abstract but extremely coherent view of the physical universe that was premised on building up all of nature from a small number of elements and forces. These scientists uncovered the very roots of that world and exposed them for the culture of the Western world to absorb, adopt, and emulate. It was culturally clear from these discoveries that physics was the pinnacle of human intellectual production. It was equally clear that the physicists' contention that understanding of human circumstance might best be achieved by understanding the elemental foundations of phenomena would become the dominant mode of human thought. And so it did. It is within this general intellectual background that the technological ideas of Villa Savoye emerged.

Villa Savoye represents the uncovering of the elemental particles of architecture just as the atom uncovered the elemental particles of nature. Instead of the variety of forms of matter being built up from combinations of protons, electrons, and neutrons, the form of buildings was proposed to be built up of horizontal slabs, vertical piers, and walls. Unlike the notion of the atom, however, these fundamental elements derive their power to constitute the whole of the possibility of the built world not because they have discovered the mechanics of the underlying structure of architecture but because they uncover an ideal formal basis for the development of architectural meaning. The slab proposes the boundaries of domain. The wall defines separation and connection. The pier is the form that separates slabs from the earth so that the essential conditions of a habitable space might be achieved. Each identifies an elemental portion of the definition of a self-conscious human ability to intellectually reorder material to produce a place of human habitation. Walls separate so that openings in them might selectively reconnect interior and exterior domains. The slab holds human beings within its confines. It is emblematic of all in architecture that creates the variety of forms that enclose for human purposes. The essence of the pier is not only to transmit the gravitational forces gathered by the slab to the foundation but more fundamentally to bring order to the possibility of human dwelling that has been presented by this separation.

The infinite variety of the forms and meanings of buildings is proposed to be the outcome of the assembly of these fundamental elements. As in the atom, the unique character of specific works of architecture is the outcome of the specific shape and placement of these elements one to the other. Various combinations and permutations of these elemental variables are thought to propose second-level architectural constructs such as center and edge, bottom and top, and inside and outside. These secondary constructs structure a tertiary set of seminal architectural ideas that include the garden, the room, the front, and the entry. These three levels of thought are manipulated through a process of making distinctions and relations that become the whole of a building. The meaning of each of these elements is thus both innate and relational. Each is premised on ideal architectural distinction, but the specific articulation of a design is premised on exactly how forms as ideas relate to each other and to the whole. In this sense, early modern architecture represents a kind of Greek atomism. Villa Savoye is a working out of the essential ideas of this proposal of architectural atomism in a mature design.

Building Description

The house is a large 60' X 75' rectangle with three floors of living space. The first floor is devoted to a driveway, garage, entry, and servants' quarters. The second floor contains all the major family living areas including the living room, dining room, kitchen, guest bedroom and bath, and master bedroom, bath, study, terrace, and two light courts. The first of these is a large space that connects directly to the living room and the master bedroom terrace, and the second is a small enclosed space off the kitchen. The third floor is given completely over to a small roof garden. Each floor is connected by a ramp that rises through the center of the house.

CLIMATE AND SUNLIGHT

Poissy is located approximately 20 miles northeast of Paris at 48 degrees north latitude. The climate of this area of France is continental. Winter temperatures range from average lows of 34°F to average highs of 43°F in January. Summer highs average 76°F, and lows average 58°F in July. Minimum extreme temperatures in the winter have reached 4°F in February, and extreme maximum temperatures have reached 104°F in July. The relative humidity varies from 54 to 82 percent.

At 48 degrees north latitude, the sun rises at 50 degrees east of south and sets at 50 degrees west of south on December 21. On June 21 it rises at 125 degrees east of south and sets at 125 degrees west of south. The altitude of the sun at noon on December 21 is 18 degrees; at noon on June 21 it is 63 degrees.

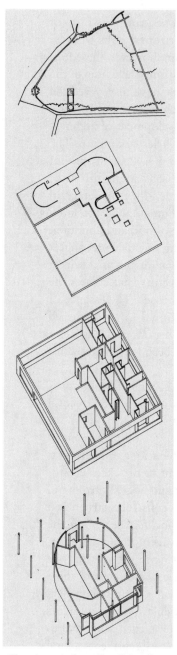

Site plan, roof garden, living floor, and ground floor of Villa Savoye.

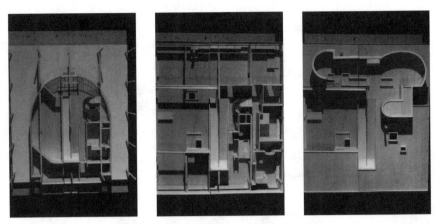

Models of the three floors of Villa Savoye.

The Mechanics of Technological Form

The mechanics of the frame, envelope, and openings for sunlight of Villa Savoye are an unusual assortment of forms when taken individually. The frame consists of reinforced columns, dropped beams, and flat slabs. The columns extend through the first two floors of the dwelling and are most often 10-inch-diameter cylinders in section, but interior columns may assume a variety of shapes. The columns are spanned by a series of one-way beams that run in an east and west direction. These beams may be incorporated in walls, dropped below the slab that they support, or may be formed within the slab as a metal pan that contains extra steel reinforcing bars. The slab itself is 6 inches thick and contains metal reinforcing top and bottom. The columns are arranged along a series of beams that are 15 feet apart except in the center of the slab where the central beam has been bifurcated to create the opening for the ramp that ascends from the ground floor to the roof terrace.

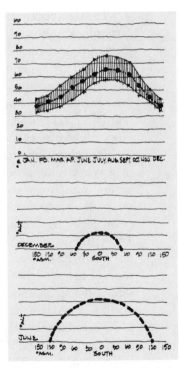

Villa Savoye's climate is typical of a continental location.

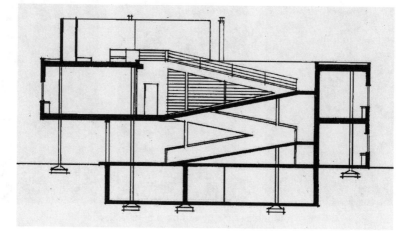

Section of Villa Savoye.

The weather envelope of the structure consists primarily of con-crete block and single glazed windows. On the ground floor, the form of this weather enclosure is a rectangle with a round end. On the second (living) floor, it is made up of an assortment of rooms or-ganized around the perimeter of the rectangle that marks the boundaries of this floor of the house. There is a wall on the third (garden terrace) floor, but it does not enclose a climatized space. None of the surfaces is insulated in any way.

Sunlight is admitted to the interior of the dwelling in a range of ways. On the ground floor, the entry is wrapped by floor-to-ceiling transparent glass. The glazing of the servants' quarters is a series of east-facing jalousie windows. The second floor is sur-rounded by walls that have a continuous horizontal slit in them. This is Le Corbusier's famous horizontal window that constitutes one of his Five Points of Architecture. The space within the walls is opened to sunlight from above by a large light court on the south side of the second floor and by a small enclosed light court on the north side. Glazing from the living room to the large south light court is full height. A punched window looks out from the master study to the large light court. The master bath is lit entirely by sky-lights from above. The wall of the roof garden has a punched win-dow in it that is on axis with the ramp that occupies the center of the house.

Analysis of Technological Form

THE SLAB, THE EARTH, AND THE SKY

The formal manipulation of technology in this house is initiated by the placement of two slabs at even intervals above the earth. These two slabs create three domains. The lowermost of the domains is located between the earth and the underside of the first slab. The earth represents the fecundity of nature and provides the domain of all living things. The uppermost of the domains exists between the upper surface of the second slab and the sky. This domain is contiguous with all of the objects that reside in the heavens, and like the Christian angels, its light communicates directly between a distant, abstract, and seemingly immutable context and the immediacy of a tangible and mutable earth. The middle domain is contained between the upper surface of the lower slab and the undersurface of the upper slab. It is a place of human mental as well as physical construction that rests between the earth and the sky but is distinct from both. If the lower domain of the house is the place where wider relations with the living world are proposed, and the upper domain is the place that probes a rich human cosmology, then the middle domain explores what a house means as a place in which to reside with other people.

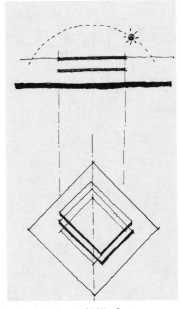

The two slabs of Villa Savoye initiate the design by creating three domains.

THE COLUMN AND GEOMETRIC ORDER

The perimeter of these two slabs is framed by sixteen evenly spaced, slender, cylindrical columns, five on each side. These five columns create a sixteen-square, 60' x 60' plan. The center of this square is a point that subdivides the square plan into four smaller squares. Nature organizes its forms as the organic outcome of the interaction of forces. In the shape of a sand dune can be read the forces of wind, water, and the weight of the sand itself that have interacted over time to create the form of the dune that exists now only to be continuously transformed by the ongoing interaction of these forces.

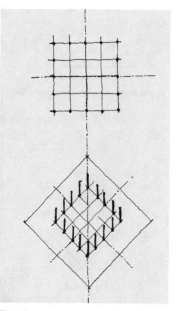

The sixteen evenly spaced perimeter columns of Villa Savoye identify the corners and midpoint of each side of a square.

The square made by the perimeter sixteen columns of Villa Savoye stands in opposition to this kind of order. The pattern that they mark is permanent, unchanging, and uniquely recognized by human intelligence as self-conscious form. The sixteen perimeter columns of Villa Savoye represent the power of the human mind to organize material rationally as counterpoint to nature's ability to organize it organically.

RATIONAL AND EMPIRICAL FORM

The shape of these columns seeks a mechanical truth. They make little attempt to be molded by, or to shape, perceptual ideals. Rather, their uniform round slender section speaks of a kind of mechanical idealism. They are the utilitarian size rather than the perceptual shape that they need to be to carry the loads from above. Their slenderness speaks of their composite construction of concrete and steel rather than the piling up of stone of a Greek column. They meet the slab and the ground without the benefit of a formal transition as base or capital. They are reduced to a pure geometric cylinder just as the slab was reduced to a pure geometric plane. In this idealized form, they represent a strange but forceful discourse between rational thought as manifest in their spatial organization and contemporary technological prowess as manifest in their size and shape.

TWO-WAY COLUMNS AND ONE-WAY BEAMS

These columns are not spanned by a two-way system of beams that might be expected to grow out of their square order. Instead the enclosure of the house is spanned by five one-way beams. At the south and north edges of the building, this one-way beam system extends beyond the limits of the original square in conformance with the mechanical propensities of this structural system. This extension is initiated by cantilevering the two large beams that serve as the east and west boundaries of the second floor of the house and continuing

The perimeter columns of Villa Savoye are classically placed but are unadorned, slender cylinders, reflecting a technological stance of the twentieth century.

the pattern of this extension in the cantilever of the remainder of the internal one-way beams. The outcome is a rectangular floor plate of the second floor that contains within its bounds the rational order of a square of columns that initiated the ground floor.

THE CONDITIONAL COLUMN

The ordered configuration of sixteen perimeter columns stands in contrast to the order of the internal columns of the design. Instead of being organized in a rational pattern, these columns slide along one-way beams so that they continue to support the slab above but do so in a manner that fulfills local pragmatic requirements of the plan without reinforcing the geometric order that was initiated by

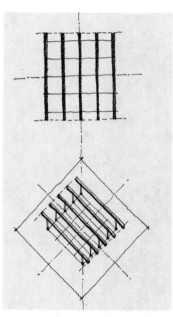

The house is spanned by five one-way beams.

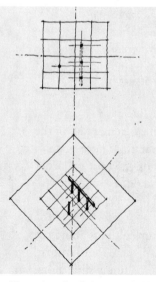

These interior columns of Villa Savoye are placed where local conditions require them to be.

the sixteen perimeter columns. These conditional columns take the shape that their local circumstance calls for. They may be cylindrical like the perimeter columns or may become square in section or be encased in the form of a wall that intersects them. Their genesis is no longer the order of geometry of classical Greece but has become the prosaic order of a utilitarian twentieth-century pragmatic industrial culture. They do what needs to be done in the most direct and least self-conscious way.

This second arrangement of columns sets up a kind of formal dialogue with the first. It suggests that the column has a dual responsibility to the plan. On one hand, its obligation is to support the slab but to be suppressed in terms of its own capacity to bring order to the plan. On the other, not only does it support the slab, but its shape and placement become dominant constituents of the order of space. Each kind of column confronts the other with what it is not and in so doing signifies the difference between structural elements that create spatial order and those that manifest situational order. The contention that the mechanical needs of support preceded the will of the column to bring order to constructed space would seem to be transposed in this design. The dialogue of rational and circumstantial columns in Villa Savoye strongly suggests that the first duty of the column was to bring order to nature by creating patterns of space that could easily be grasped by the human mind. The task of providing mere support, though necessary, becomes a secondary concern of the columns of Villa Savoye.

RATIONAL AND CONDITIONAL COLUMNS AS THE CENTER

These two kinds of columns meet at the center of the house. The one-way beam system makes no space for the ramp to ascend at the center of the two horizontal floor slabs. To create such a space, the mid-portion of the central beam is divided into two beams and separated so that a void is left through which the ramp can penetrate the floor. The columns that frame this ramp maintain the logic of the one-way beam system of the interior of the plan, as they do not conform to the position that would be suggested that they take by the perimeter columns. Columns slide along the bifurcated beam at the perimeter of the ramp void until they occupy positions at the ends and centerpoint of these beams. In this way, the relation of the perimeter col-

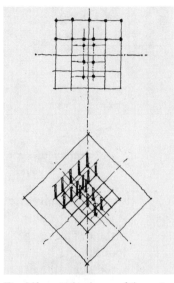

The bifurcated column of the entry is extended to create the center void for the ramp.

umns at the edge of the house is reversed at its center. At the edge, a rectangular plan boundary holds a square of columns within it. At the center, a rectangular plan form centers a square and orders the columns that bound it to mark its center.

If the columns of the perimeter of the building had been organized in a manner that allowed this void to occur without further design maneuvers, the opportunity to create center as space out of order that specifies center as point would have disappeared. Center as a special human concern would have become center as the organic outcome of a spatial system. No effort would have been needed to create this special place in a system that did not initially admit to its presence, and hence the opportunity to call out its distinction through creation would have been diminished. The opportunity to mark the center as the reconciliation of the rational square and one-way beam systems confers a significance on this form that can only grow from design manipulation as intellectual intent.

THE COLUMN AS THE ENTRY

Inside the first rank of columns at the west end of the house lies a second rank of columns that take issue with the prosaic order that

The entry to Villa Savoye.

is more generally established by the internal one-way beam system of the interior of the house. They line up exactly with the columns of the perimeter that flank them. This double rank of columns lies opposite the side of the house that is approached by automobile, but it is the side of the house that contains the entry on the ground floor and the living room on the second floor. Architectural convention requires a formality in these two spaces of a house that has less to do with the more pragmatic ideas that might provide the impetus for the organization of a bathroom or kitchen. The entry contains the sense of what the front of a building connects to and hence how it confronts its context. This kind of formal arrangement of elements is often assumed to have an obligation to a larger community in architecture. The way in which people tend to formally address their larger context attempts to maintain patterns that are understood by that community. The second rank of columns of Villa Savoye's front facade performs that task. They create the idea of the front of the building in their allegiance to the geometric order of the perimeter columns of the house. The beam that extends from the center column of this second rank of columns to the beam between the two columns that mark the beginning of the ramp announces the transformation of line into void that will become the entry to the house. The continuation of this formally ordered second rank of columns through the midlevel of the house designates the difference between the communal living areas and the remaining, more personally inhabited areas of this floor. This organization of columns allows the living room to reverse its orientation at this level so that its front might now face the large interior light court as the formal abstraction of the front yard of the house.

COLUMN AND BEAM AS FRONT, BACK, AND SIDE

The one-way beams atop the square perimeter of columns produce a building boundary of two different lengths. In so doing they have created a distinction that connotes the front, back, and sides of the dwelling. What might be traditionally called the facade of a building is the outcome of this distinction. On the ground floor, this facade is composed of equally spaced columns alone. On the third floor, the facade is created by a single wall in the absence of columns. The facade of the second floor weaves together these two architectural elements. The sides of the house are created by columns and beams with a continuous horizontal space between them that forms the boundary wall of the house. Columns intersect these wall beams in a way that maintains formal independence of both, but in a manner that also allows

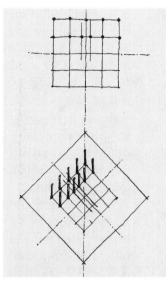

The second row of columns repeats the order of the sixteen perimeter columns of the house to identify its front.

each to become what neither can accomplish alone. The distinction between the square of the columns and the rectangle of the beams

Model of the front and side of Villa Savoye.

is remembered in this facade by the opaque panels at each end of the east and west sides of the house. The north and south front and back facades are created by the same weaving of beam and column, but without the cantilever. They present a facade that grows directly from the pure, rational square that initiated the house. Their formal origin remains unmodified by the rectangular form of the one-way beam system. This formal distinction between pure and geometrically impure order forges the difference between the facade of the house that faces the greater community to become a part of its vocabulary of pattern and facades that might take on their own local organization.

THE BOTTOM AND THE TOP AS BOUNDARIES OF THE IN-BETWEEN

The ground floor and the roof garden create boundaries of the conditions of climatic enclosure and openings for sunlight that will be developed in the living midsection of the house. The ground floor enclosure is withdrawn from the edge of the building by 15 feet on three sides. It is completely enclosed by a combination of glazed and opaque walls. Inhabitants of this enclosure receive only diffuse sunlight that has been reflected from the ground. They are too far recessed from the edge of the building to receive direct sunlight. They look out from a completely enclosed space onto a horizontal context that is directly illuminated by sunlight. The enclosure of the

Sectional photograph of Villa Savoye model.

roof garden consists of a single wall. There is no climatic inside or outside of this space, only an announcement of the architectural form that is capable of creating this distinction. The form of this wall is directly and completely exposed to every change in the luminescent conditions of the sky. It reflects these changes exactly.

The polar conditions that state the building envelope to be completely enclosed versus completely open and directly versus diffusely sunlit space are a way of stating the seminal conditions of human inhabitation on the earth under the sky. These technological boundaries begin to serve as abstractions that are central to the ability of people to locate themselves in nature by making such distinctions. Enclosure is initiated by the wall but consists of the entire range of ways in which buildings mediate between people and how they feel the air. Sunlight illuminates objects directly or indirectly. The first kind of reflection grants orientation and time; the second does not. The single wall of the roof garden seen in the sky is paired with the completed enclosure of the ground floor that is seen with the earth. Villa Savoye states these primary architectural distinctions as the abstractions of constructed form so that they might be manipulated as ideas.

BOUNDARY AS HORIZON

The in-between or middle domain of the house then becomes the juncture where these propositions are formally explored. The

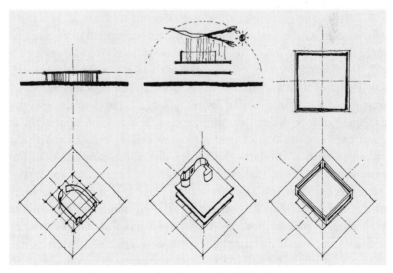

Boundaries of each domain of Villa Savoye.

middle condition of climate and sunlight is first marked by the wall that encloses this space. This wall with its continuous horizontal opening is the constructed boundary of the house as its own site as paired with the natural boundary of the building site as the horizon. It is the horizon where the air, earth, and sky meet to create the broadest definition of the natural human domain. The earth, air, and sky merge in the horizontal slit that encircles the living floor of Villa Savoy as it looks beyond this formal abstraction to link it to its analogous condition in the natural world. This wall and its horizontal slit become the intellectual abstraction of the horizon that forges the extent of the domain of Villa Savoye.

BOUNDARY WALL PLUS LIGHT COURT VERSUS LIGHT COURT

Two light courts are placed within this boundary. The first of these is a large open area bounded to the south by the horizon wall, to the west by the floor-to-ceiling glazing of the living room, to the north by the translucent glass block of the ramp, and to the east by the punched window of the study and the covered but otherwise open exposure of the master bedroom terrace. Every possible condition of architectural spatial communication except that of complete opacity is represented around this court. Opacity is reserved for the small light court that adjoins the kitchen. It is completely surrounded by opaque walls with the exception of the horizon wall that forms its north boundary.

The floor of each light court is analogous to the reorganization of the earth as the garden. Both light courts invite the sky and climate into the dwelling space of the house from above as does a garden, but having done so, they each treat this light and air differently. The larger of the two frames the light court with various degrees of transparency and in so doing invites adjoining spaces to share in the garden and in the sky to varying degrees. The second, opaque light court captures the sky for itself; it shares this light and air with no adjoining spaces. It relates the garden directly to the sky. As in the case of the columns, each makes the other what it is by specifying what it is not. The small light court is a place that states the relation of the sky to the earth in the singularity of condition that might exist purely between these two major markers of human location in time and in place. The large light court develops the richness of exchange that might be had in exploring the range of communication

that light and air might forge between the conditions tha
call the inside and the outside of a house.

CLIMATE AS DEFINITIONS OF OUTSIDE AND INSIDE

The relationship of climatic spaces that is created by the boundaries
of the house extends from the outsideness of the territory beyond the
walls of the house to the most interior of the spaces of the dwelling,
located in the master bathroom. Between these two poles exist a range
of climatic boundaries that tell of the complexity with which human
beings inhabit the climate. The space outside the boundary wall of the
house is the outside/outside. It is just as clearly divided from the interi-
or domain of the house by this wall as it is mediated with that domain
through the spaces between the columns of the first floor and merged
with it in the uncontrolled climate of the roof garden of the third
floor. In the outside/outside, the climate is neither physically controlled by human intervention nor capable of being probed and manipulated as an idea. It lies outside the human domain because it has
not been converted by human construction into a set of symbols that
might be interpreted and manipulated by human intelligence.

The two light courts are characterized by the same empirical climatic conditions as those that exist outside/outside, but these conditions have now been captured within the boundaries of the horizon
wall. This new climate is that of the outside/inside. The outside/
inside remains physically undifferentiated from the climate of nature
but has now become a part of the formally malleable idea structure
of the dwelling.

The covered master terrace that lies along one side of the larger
light court is sheltered from moisture but open to temperature
change and to the wind. It is mirrored by the living room with the
exception that the transparent glazing that stands between this
room and the light court can be closed so that different climatic
comfort conditions can be maintained inside this space. The kitchen
and bedrooms have climatic contact with the outside only through
sliding windows that fill the horizontal slit of the outer walls of
these rooms. Each is an example of the inside/inside. And finally
there is the master bath, which has no climatic contact with the outside at all. It lies within the rooms that lie within the boundary of
the house. It is protected from the vagaries of climate by these layers
of space. It represents the inside/inside/inside.

The house might, in fact, be seen as a center that extends outward from the personal enclosedness of the master bath to the abstraction of the wall that surrounds the house as the boundary of the inside to the outsideness of the natural horizon. Or it might be considered in reverse as the creation of a set of boundaries that emanate from the sense of climate that begins with the complete uncontrolledness of the touch of nature to finally reach their conclusion in the tactile withdrawal of space from contact with the natural climate in the insideness of the master bath. These are not as much a range of possible physical conditions as they are a set of ideas with which human beings define how they are in the natural world of the air. It is a richly symbolic placement, as is manifest in the wall of the roof garden, but it is also a richly tactile placement, as is established by the enclosure of the ground floor entry lobby.

NATURAL LIGHT IN THE MIDDLE DOMAIN

Sunlight is defined in Villa Savoye by the openings of the building as illumination that is admitted from the side and hence connects the interior with the landscape and as light that is received from above and hence connects human existence with the sky. The light from the sky is direct; form is seen in this light as the spontaneous reflection of the light of the sky unmediated by other forms. Horizontal light, conversely, is seen in the reflection of other things on the

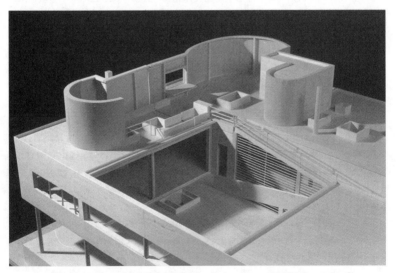

Model photograph of the major light court of Villa Savoye.

earth. It links the domain of things together through their mutual reflection of the sun. Two categories of form are thus created. The first of these is the category of form that is a direct reflection of sunlight within the boundaries of the dwelling. The second is light that has been reflected by objects outside the domain and is being appropriated by the domain through an opening.

The horizontal opening that bands the house captures the horizon as the most distant boundary of a human domain as an edited strip. It is like the Magritte painting of a landscape mounted on a canvas in front of a window that is also a painting of the same landscape. The horizon that is captured by the second-floor strip window of Villa Savoye is the actual horizon as portrayed within the abstraction of that horizon that forms the boundary of the dwelling as analogous to that of nature. Sunlight animates the forms of the natural world, and sunlight establishes its extent. So it is with the abstract horizon formed by the horizontal exterior windows of Villa Savoye. The reflected light of the objects in the landscape that are captured by this opening is paired with the objects within this domain that are seen via the same vehicle.

The two light courts of the middle domain capture the direct sun in a manner that complements the way in which it is captured by the objects of the roof garden. The objects of the roof garden are thrust into the light of the sky. The light courts receive that same light by taking it into their boundaries. They make the sky a part of the constructed domain by framing it within a constructed condition. This act of capturing allows a natural event, the sky, to become part of a lexicon of human meaning. The uncaptured sky remains a part of the natural world, one that can be inhabited but not symbolically manipulated and hence remains unavailable to human interpretation.

The windows of the second-floor rooms that surround these courtyards, with the exception of the bathroom, all capture a kind of horizontal light. The living room and the terrace of the master bedroom both are transparent to the central court while being flanked by the light of the horizon. They reverse the transparency of the ground floor because they look inward at the direct light of the sky instead of looking outward at the reflected light of the earth. The only difference between the two is that the former sees east light from the court and west light from the horizon, and the terrace sees west light from the court and east light from the horizon. In this difference of similarities exists the fundamental property of the sun's ability to locate human existence in space and in time. The window of the bedroom study sees the same light as does the master bedroom terrace rather than as a transparent space but as a framed view. The difference is one of the distance created by the presumption of passage. The light court is a possible place of inhabitation to one while it is an inaccessible garden of objects much like those of the outside world of nature to the other. This interpretation is reinforced by the similarly shaped window in the wall in the roof garden. This window too appropriates the horizontal light of the reflected natural world by framing it. The frame of this window again distances the reflected world that it captures. The small light court is bounded on three sides by opaque walls and hence is seen not to be a part of the living domain but rather to be united with the horizon and the sky, which its openings enframe. The last of the light rooms is, as in the case of climate, the master bathroom. This room receives only the light of the sky through a small skylight in the ceiling. Unlike the roof garden, this opening admits only a small framed vision of the sky into the room and hence distances the objects of the sky just as punched horizontal openings do.

Each of these relationships comes into being only as the sun rises on the eastern horizon and dies in the darkness of the sunset. Each is given a place in space through an orientation created by the passage of the sun and a place in time through this passage. The connections that Villa Savoye forges with the natural world that it inhabits are thus cosmic in character. Elements that might assume

The master bath as the inside/inside/inside of the house.

central importance in other designs are simply attached to this structure as secondary decoration. The hearth, the wash basin, and the table, although specifying important social architectural constructs in the design of other houses, become tangential at best in the design lexicon of Villa Savoye. It is the earth and the sky that forge the ground of the design vocabulary of this house, and it is sunlight that brings both into being as the boundary of human dwelling in this work.

Technological Form as Metaphorical Thought

Elemental technological forms are manipulated in this design to produce and probe seminal architectural constructs that are more often defined representationally in other works of architecture. The facade is the product of weaving together the logic of the boundary of the roof garden and that of the ground floor. The roof garden is created with walls alone. The ground floor boundary is made of columns alone. The middle facade of the Villa Savoye becomes the self-conscious intersection of wall and column. Column and beam identify front and side. The horizontal light of the horizon that connects all things on the earth and the vertical light of the sky that names them are fused in the light courts that structure the plan of the living floor of the house. The entry of the house is located by a central column but becomes a passage by assuming the attitude of the bifurcated beam that forms the void for the central ramp. Front and back are denoted by ranks of columns. The central ramp is a passage through domains. Its initiation on the earth is extended through the creation of the new, abstract earth of the light court to link both with the sky. The boundedness of the enclosure of the ground floor is contrasted with the enclosure of the wall on the roof terrace, which states but does not consummate this possibility. Horizon is restated as the product of constructed form. Edge and center are both the product of the rational placement of columns. The domain becomes an intellectually coherent, compact, and highly abstract microcosm of the conditions of inhabitation found in the natural world.

Technological Metaphors as Distinctions

This kind of metaphorical treatment of technological form might be called *discursive distinctions*. Three underlying assumptions link mechanics to meaning in this architectural construct. The first of these is that the world of architectural meaning is built up from a very few fundamental technological elements. The origin of these elements is their ability to modify the natural world because the initial problem of architecture was found in that modification. These elemental technological forms are indivisible because their task was not reducible to more fundamental constituent tasks. Successive layers of architectural meanings have these elements as their underlying structure, and so the essential ideas of architecture might be deduced from an analysis of complex architectural constructions as the outcome of the shapes and relations of basic elements. The ideal underlying form of the slab places human beings in relation to the earth and to the sky. The underlying ideal form of the column marks out the territory that is to be organized by the human mind as opposed to that which is to be organized by unmediated natural force. Walls and openings forge relationships between the outside and inside. From these abstractions, the plethora of architectural types and styles emerges.

The second assumption is that these elements are capable of creating the meanings of inhabitation not because of their inherent characteristics but because of their position with regard to other elements. The column achieves the status of creating a meaningful construct of dwelling not because it has a special kind of capital or proportional shape but because it is placed in certain ways with other columns, slabs, beams, and walls. The primary technological function of the column, to separate slabs from the earth so that the space of dwelling might come into being, is the only universal qualification of this element for selection as an elemental architectural form. Slabs are placed horizontally to become floors or ceilings. They might be punctured in any of an infinite variety of ways or may be placed in specific relation to columns to create an infinite array of ideas of enclosure. The only fundamental obligation of the slab is to separate in order to distinguish domains. Walls are vertical. They confront inhabitants in the upright posture that typifies the way in which people identify their location in the world.

Finally, this kind of elementalism would be no different than the atomism of early-twentieth-century physics if it did not treat the placement of the human mind and body within the structures created by building up elements differently than does physics. In physics, the myriad substances that form the human context are the outcome of the combinative characteristics of the elements themselves. In a discourse of distinctions, this is not so. Even the most complex architectural assemblages of the column and the slab would remain mute if they did not place human beings with regard to the earth and the sky in meaningful ways. Inhabitation, in this sense, is not the product of the composition of architectural elements but more fundamentally the way in which elements place a person in the natural world. It is this power to locate by positioning people with regard to the earth and sky that is the goal of this form of architectural reasoning. This power is discursively discovered so that it might be discursively conveyed.

The dialectics of elemental idealism that are the outcome of this formal discourse are a highly intellectual and abstract mode of making metaphors of human existence from the mechanics of architectural technology. Their base as a limited set of fundamental architectural technologies requires that buildings be analytically reduced to seminal ideas. This is a difficult but apparently compelling intellectual search in all fields of contemporary human thought. Its contention is that such basic constructs lie at the foundation of all human ideas to be discovered by the most rigorous and insightful of intellectual inspections. The relational logic of discursive distinctions is that of any complex symbolic system. All discursive symbols garner the specificity of their meaning from their position with regard to other symbols. They do so by specifying and relating distinctions.

This kind of relational interpretation of meaning creates a complementary reasoning process. The formal symbol in question gains its specific meaning from its context but also bequeaths on that context the ability to state a particular idea. Hence in Villa Savoye the columns of the perimeter become the boundary of the house because of the pattern they create one with the other in relation to columns that do not assume this pattern. The absence of direct sunlight on the ground floor allows it to name objects of the roof terrace as being linked to the sky. The inside/outside of the light courts allows the inside/inside/inside of the master bath to be understood as a distinction of human habitation. In each instance, the manipulation of technological form depends on its reduction to an elemental state so that the seminal ideas of human inhabitation might be reestablished from that base with intellectual rigor. Few buildings can match Villa Savoye for pure intellectual prowess. Its intellectual abstractions, like those of the thought of early-twentieth-century physics on which they are modeled, reveal a universal and coherent vision of the foundations of all architecture.

Conclusion: Metaphorical Technology

Nature. A creative agent, force, or principle in the universe acting as a creative guiding intelligence: a set of principles held to be established for the regulation of the universe or observed in its operation.

Technology. The science of the application of knowledge to practical purposes.

Metaphor. One kind of object or idea in place of another to suggest a likeness or analogy between them.
Webster's Third New International Dictionary, 1968

This book has grown from the suspicion that there is more to architectural technology than might be literally measured. The analysis of the technological qualities of the houses in the previous four chapters begins to specify what this "more" might be. These interpretations assume that technology in architecture can be seen in a different light: that nature can be understood as felt force manifest in architectural form. The kinds of ideas that emerge from this analysis are directed primarily toward designers and their need for operative design thought. They couch the interpretation of the responses of these houses to gravity, climate, and sunlight in terms that might initiate formal investigations of these issues.

This analysis is specific to these four houses. It will remain an anecdotal vision of architectural technology if it cannot be demonstrated to be capable of generating a more general set of principles. If the analysis of these four houses is to lay the base for such generalizations, they will be required to specify a metaphoric connection between technology as "the application of knowledge to practical purposes" and how people understand nature as "creative agent, force, or principle in the universe acting as a creative guiding intelligence." The ideas that serve to connect these seemingly disparate categories of thought must grow from an understanding of technologies of habitation. The objective of this final chapter is to begin to outline this more general connection.

The thrust of this exploration has been to begin to develop an understanding of the possible contribution of technology to metaphorical rather than empirical thought in architecture. This focus is intended not to deny the contributions of technology to the measurable utility of buildings but to broaden the architectural question of the role of technology in architectural design and ultimately in the meaning manifest in the buildings that these designs specify. The center of this issue grows from the idea that architectural technology is housed in architectural form and that form is capable of initiating qualitative as well as quantitative interpretation. The quantitative analysis of architectural technology is relatively well developed. It requires no strong advocate to advance its case in the discipline of architecture. Strangely, the qualitative aspects of this form are not nearly as well understood. Perhaps it is simply too easy to reduce formal architectural problems to those of composition and of economics. Much workaday architecture is considered in this way. But beneath conventional manipulations of architectural form in the "business" of design remains the sense that good buildings deliver more than compositional pleasure or economic efficiencies. Buildings that are maintained to present the best of what architecture accomplishes are assumed to be able to sustain analysis: they are assumed to propose architectural ideas.

Formal Comparisons of the Four Houses

A more general outline of the kind of vocabulary and the logic of the formal organization of the technologies of these houses is made apparent in a comparison of how their floors, walls, roofs, frames, and openings locate people in nature.

FLOORS AND RELATIONSHIPS TO THE EARTH

The floor of the Finnish log farmhouse is two feet above grade. The floor of Orinda is located at the level of the ground. The Wall House superimposes a floor as a bridge in the air independent of the vagaries of the earth against a floor that follows the contours of the earth to mingle with its virtues. Villa Savoye uses the floor to separate the idea of domain into categories that relate human existence to being held between the earth and the sky. In each of these cases, the floor separates people from the cold and damp ground, but in so doing, each places these inhabitants in a special relation to the earth. The being above of the Finnish log cabin, the being continuous with the terrain of Orinda, the being with the earth and floating above it of the Wall House, and the being placed between the earth and sky of Villa Savoye are all ways in which human beings reference their own existence to that which surrounds them. The floor has a special obligation in this regard because it not only provides a surface of the envelope that separates inhabitants from damp and cold conditions but simultaneously provides the surface that they stand on. In so doing, a particular act of standing is referenced to all other acts of standing as a means to take mental as well as physical possession of territory.

WALLS AS SEPARATION AND CONNECTION

The walls of each house similarly convey different attitudes with regard to their task of separating inhabitants from outdoor climates. The walls of the Finnish log farmhouse are thick and heavy and are punctured only where requirements for light or entry demand that they be penetrated. The walls of Orinda are just the opposite. They are thin, light, and punctured by relatively enormous openings that damage their ability to discretely enclose space. The walls of the Wall House are writ as individual entities, part of the ensemble of the house but also distinct from it as forms unto themselves. Those of the Villa Savoye explore the ways in which a wall is construed mentally to be a boundary. The log farmhouse wall powerfully excludes the landscape to delimit the territory of the hearth. Those of Orinda allow the wall's ability to exclude to be dominated by the ability of its absence to include that which surrounds the house. The walls of the Wall House symbolically exclude the prosaic world at its edges and honorifically include the natural landscape at its center. Those of Villa Savoye build a microcosm of the world at large as an abstract mental conception manifest in material form. In each case, the physical wall initiates mental abstraction of the way in which people think about how the worlds of things and of ideas are conceptually divided and reconnected selectively.

ROOFS AND RELATIONSHIPS TO THE SKY

The roof of each house covers its occupants from the sky. Three of these roofs have an apex at their center, and one does not. One is completely opaque to the sky; three are not. Villa Savoye is the only one of these houses to have a flat roof. In fairness to the intent of this design, it might be more accurate to say that it has no roof at all, but only a series of floors, one piled atop the other. The only real roof of this dwelling is, in fact, the sky that covers the roof garden and the courtyards enclosed below. The Finnish farmhouse, conversely, is completely covered from the sky above. The space between the cupped ceiling and the ridged roof is as thick a protection against the sky as the space below the floor is to the ground and the thick walls are to the air. The Wall House and Orinda both separate inhabitants from the sky, but both also reestablish the relationship of the ceiling to the sky as opening and as formal referent. The skylight that centers the ceiling of Orinda is restated as the center of the plan of the Wall House in the opening of the courtyard to the sky. As the ridge beam of Orinda bisects its skylight, suggesting the relationship between the center constructed by humans and that created by nature, so too does the locating frame of the Wall House run through the courtyard opening to the sky. Each roof serves the same utilitarian purpose, yet each forges a different relationship with the cosmos in the particularities of the specific form that it takes.

FRAMES AS CONCEPTS OF ORDER

The frame of each house resists gravity, but again, the form that this resistance takes is very different in each. In the Finnish log farmhouse, the frame manifests a complex pattern of hierarchical order that emanated from the trial-and-error placing of branches and logs in spanning this single-room house. That of the Wall House is diametrically opposed to this kind of formal order of the frame. Not only are differences in loads not picked out by the members of this frame, but little is done to distinguish between the way in which these loads are gathered and brought to the ground. Beams and columns are of the same material and general cross section independent of their structural task. The order of the frame of the Wall House is rational: it superimposes a mental construct on empirical necessity. That of the farmhouse is empirical: it develops a mental construct of order from the way in which phenomena are observed to occur in the world of natural force. The outside columns of Villa Savoye are rational and universal. The inside columns are specific to their location and conditional. The frame of the roof of Orinda is a pragmatic reminder of the efficiencies of mass production. The columns of Orinda are referential. They formally identify what is a special activity within the house with a form that has an architectural history of proclaiming that which is significant against a background of that which is not. Each frame suggests a different conception of the origin and duties of the architectural concept of the rooted order of the earth. None can be set aside as trivial or less insightful than its counterparts because each conveys a vision of that order that is important to the ways in which people have attempted to structure the events around them.

The openings of each house illuminate its interior, but to different ends. The windows of Villa Savoye each exist to reference dwelling space to its relationship to the earth and sky. Each particular opening of the house distances, gathers, represents, and relates a specific notion of how sunlight creates a place within a house as the result of a horizontal or vertical opening that admits direct or reflected sunlight. In the Finnish log farmhouse, this task is far more prosaically presented. Light from the windows, a precious commodity in the harsh winter, is meted out discreetly. This same discretion is transformed by the windows of the Wall House into openings that reveal the essential character of the surfaces that reflect their light. The unbroken horizontal continuity of diminishing reflections of sunlight is named by the sun to be the formal essence of wall, ceiling, and floor. That same continuity of enclosure might be seen against the transparency of the courtyard, which invites the sky and the landscape into the center of the dwelling. Orinda is more interested in the quality of horizontal sunlight as a human reference to time and orientation, as opposed to the sky vault's lack of the same, than to any functional use of this light. In each case, sunlight gathers a commodity into the dwelling that would be absent had the opening not been shaped and related to other architectural elements in exactly the manner that it is. This is not a general kind of relationship but rather one with specific goals. Simply illuminating a surface with a measurable amount of sunlight would hardly qualify the use of this natural force as one that probes its potential meaning to human beings.

To claim a purely quantifiable view of technology's role in buildings would mean that the formal interpretations brought forth in the analysis of the four study houses, or of any other formal use of architectural technology, would have to be dismissed as a technological issue. Speculation concerning the relation of technological elements to the forces that they manipulate would be truncated. Architects would no longer be able to ask if there are meaningful differences between the horizontal axis of the earth and the vertical axis of the sky in terms of how people view their place in nature. They would no longer be able to probe the order of gravity as the foundation of symbolic spatial patterns. They would no longer be able to examine the role of the changing of the seasons in relation to the passing of a human life. The matter of time would no longer be reflected in sunlight. No longer would an image of the cosmos be appropriate grounds for generating and interpreting technological form in buildings.

Speculation about the relational ideas created by technological elements would likewise have to be abandoned. All architectural thought depends not simply on the shape or size of a particular element but on the relationships that that element establishes with all of the other forms of the building. These elements cannot be wrested from their context with impunity lest they cease to have specific architectural meaning. To isolate technological elements from the fullness of the role that they might play in this creation of relational meaning would be to excise a major portion of architecture's ability to express ideas of human habitation. The role of technological elements such as the arrangement of the columns of Villa Savoye to create ideas of boundary and front, the too much of the interior columns of Orinda with the too little of the columnless corner, the mechanically incorrect square section of the beams of the Wall House, or the hierarchical order of the frame of the Finnish log farmhouse would have to be relegated to a different arena of architectural speculation than that of technology.

And finally, but perhaps most importantly, such a reduction would not serve people and the ways in which they consider their own lives. It is currently popular to reduce the human conception of the self to purely psychological or commercial terms. We are what we emote or what we choose to buy. Such proclamations may be justified, but they make such claims at the expense of the understanding that we remain substantially the human beings that we have always been. We bring the same equipment and needs to the task of living that we have always brought to this task. While portions of this task might ebb and flow in their perceived importance to us, they never fully disappear. How we occupy the world in buildings is a fundamental part of the human understanding of the significance of life. It is the way in which we as human beings most directly rearrange the forces of nature tangibly to suit human purpose.

There is and always has been a place in the human psyche that understands itself through the actions that it takes on the world outside of it and the way in which that world appears to respond. Architectural technology lies clearly in the domain of this kind of understanding of the self.

The significance of these comparisons lies in the range and kind of architectural ideas that the technological forms of these four houses are able to enunciate. There may be differences of opinion about the specific conclusions proposed by these interpretations, but the general ability of the technical form to propel such notions would appear not to be in doubt. Floors allow people to take possession of territory; walls divide the worlds of things and ideas; roofs relate existence to the cosmos, frames order our lives, and sunlight gathers a mental conception of our surroundings into our domain.

There is thus good reason to admit to the existence of architectural technology as form and of the analysis of that form to encompass a rich interweaving of empirical impact and metaphorical meaning in the world. If these comparisons of the technological elements of the four houses of this study establish anything, it is that architecture is a separate and distinct way in which human beings have come to manipulate and understand the natural world around them. This kind of understanding cannot be collapsed casually into other forms of thought because to do so does irrevocable harm to the fullness of the meaning of technological form in architecture as a symbol. The power of any set of human thinking symbols is to reveal the richness and depth of human thought and actions to human beings. To truncate the power of the symbols of architectural technology would seem to arbitrarily cut off a possibility of human understanding from ourselves.

Comparison of Technological Metaphors
The formal characteristics of the technologies of these four houses might be generalized as different ways of metaphorically portraying nature through the buildings that people create. The objective of any metaphor is to reveal a quality of an event that cannot be defined literally. Its power is to open up speculation about the human significance of these events. We have grown so used to the literal nature of science that many of us are tempted to forget that this is not the nature we actually inhabit. Nature means more to us than its reduction to quantities of mass and energy. The metaphors presented

by the technological form of the four houses are simply restatements of the ways in which we more fully understand nature as lived values. This kind of thought always lies at the heart of architectural design, whether it is overtly stated to be the case or not. We all search for the meaning of our own existence in all that we do. This search often occurs to us only when we take the time to speculate about it; a task that we seem more and more reticent to undertake. Nonetheless it is a task that none of us can avoid altogether.

NATURE AS TANGIBLE TRANSACTIONS

The Finnish log farmhouse metaphorically proposes a nature of "tangible transactions." The technology of the house suggests that the core of nature might be grasped through contemplating the ways in which it appears to work. Nature is laid bare for us in each of its physical transactions. It doesn't really matter if the transactions observed are a cell dividing, a quark leaving a vapor trail, or a beam holding up a ceiling. It is not simply a mechanical nature that is exposed in these transactions; it is a metaphysical nature. The idea of nature is revealed in the elegant ways in which it is always found to operate. Chaos, in its classic sense, is simply human ignorance of this underlying structure. The notched logs of the Finnish log cabin are tiny metaphors for this much larger belief in the inevitable elegance of nature's operational patterns. There is a singular correctness to the way in which they fit together; there is a sense of rightness to the way in which they so directly fulfill a human purpose; there is a sense of their inevitability as a solution discovered within the idea of nature as manifest in elegant patterns. We may never grasp all the rules that are the origin of these patterns, but people are repeatedly reminded of their existence by architectural technologies.

NATURE AS SENSUALLY REVEALED BELIEF

But what of the human rituals and celebrations that have always marked auspicious natural occurrences? Need nature be reduced to ideas that spring from mechanics alone, or might nature be just as powerfully presented to us as mythologies that endow these operations with special qualities? Orinda's technology may manifest a nature that reflects nature's elegant patterns, but that is not what makes the form of this house a powerful metaphor for what nature is at its heart. Nature is, in the technological form of Orinda, that which we ritualize. It is the sum of our metaphysical speculations about its magic. We never really outgrow these speculations, even though a scientific culture finds them unfashionable. These beliefs are always a part of how we understand nature because it is not simply a mindless mechanical set of actions but a purposeful and coherent actor across time. The sense that all evolution is an act of pure mechanical chance disturbs us. If nature is such a set of arbitrary actions, then people, as the highest outcome of this caprice, are no more than an accident. Even if true, this arbitrariness denies our sense of the importance of our own existence. But if there is purpose in nature and people alike, it must be driven by something beyond purposeless mechanics: it must be driven by spirit. Spirit has been our partner as our sense of ourselves and as our sense of the nature that gave birth to our species for a far longer time than has the simpler construct of nature as pure mechanism. The size, shape, and placement of Orinda's technologies remind us that spirit is encoded in our rituals. These technologies attempt to reunite us with nature as that which might be sensed to be its purpose and hence ours within it.

NATURE AS EMBEDDED ORIGINS

The technology of the Wall House as a metaphor for nature contains this same sense of spirit but finds its origins in another place. In a world so given to abstractions of the mind, there is no longer a large space for abstractions that grow from the tangible act of making things. It is as if our intellectual sophistication finds it necessary to drive our understanding of the world ever farther from that which we can touch. Real intellectual achievement seems, in the Western world, to emanate from that which we can think. We build intellectual abstractions on intellectual abstractions. The need for these abstractions to comply with our sense of ourselves in a physical world of perception and feeling is at odds with these intellectual constructions. We appear to think that arriving at the "truth," whatever that may be, depends on separating thought from being. Perhaps for some domains of human ideas, this presupposition may be necesary and helpful. But how might this be the case in the buildings that we make? Is there not in this very act of material construction a kind of knowledge that will be forever denied to a mind without a hand? Can anyone who has shaped nature to fit human purpose say that his or her understanding of the world was not being shaped at the same time? How are we to understand the world that we reside in if not through the ideas that emerge from making tangible things? The technological metaphor of the Wall House claims that these lessons are neither serendipitous nor personal. There is, within this metaphor, the contention that there is a common understanding of nature that resides in the technological forms of the house. This understanding will always be present in these forms. It stems from a direct meeting of the hand and the mind that is re-created every time the construction of an architectural technology is reenacted. Nature is contained in this making. We do not understand it directly, but indirectly through this act. Nature will never yield its secrets to direct inspection in this metaphorical construct. Direct inspection always carries with it a supposition of nature's ability to empirically verify the truth about its origin and meaning. The indirect metaphor of making suggests that this truth is not a truth at all.

NATURE AS DIALECTIC DISTINCTIONS

Finally there is a metaphor of nature to fill the needs of pure intellect. We intellectually consider the world around us by making distinctions. These distinctions are developed and understood through argument. A well-made distinction stands the test of a well-fashioned argument. It presents us with a way to "rationally" understand nature and the implications of following that understanding to logical conclusions. This is the architectural technology of Socrates. Few buildings in the history of architecture can present such a compelling argument for nature as intellectual reason as that presented by the technological form of Villa Savoye. Nature, in this construct, is what technological form is able to argue it convincingly to be. Nature is the difference between the earth and the sky. It is the difference between the bounded and the unbounded, the difference between order and expedience. Our only architectural understanding of the real underlying structure of nature is the outcome of the rigor of formal technological arguments put forth by buildings such as Villa Savoye. All else is but superficial form created on the basis of readily accepted and unexamined convention. In the columns, floors, walls, and openings of Villa Savoye lies the formal path to a reasoned architectural nature.

The metaphors for nature put forth by these four houses suggest but a few of the ways with which people have examined the significance of their place in nature through the vehicle of architectural technology. This is not a closed list. Other analysis will surely suggest other metaphors. What these four examples do portray, however, is the range of thought that such metaphors might transverse. Those of the Finnish log farmhouse emanate from literal and tangible circumstances. Those of Villa Savoye are conversely intellectual and abstract. Those of Orinda and the Wall House fall somewhere between these two poles. Each finds its power in its ability to reveal that which was only suspected before it was presented with the metaphoric insight that the technological form of each house delivers.

The importance of these insights to designers is that they enunciate questions that inevitably lie at the base of design thought. Designs for buildings do not originate either in composition or in economics, though each may condition this search. They find their origin in questions that seek the significance of our existence with each other and in nature. Metaphoric thought about the nature of nature, the character of that which has always provided the context for human existence, has always been the covert initiator of technological thought in architecture. The four kinds of metaphoric thought presented in the technologies of these four houses thus simply serve to reopen the architectural question of what constitutes the significant qualities of the nature that we inhabit.

General Characteristics of Architecture's Technological Voice as Material Form

These metaphors, in turn, are based on a more general set of assumptions. These assumptions seek to identify what is essential about the act of metaphor formation itself as a ground for generating the meaning of architectural technology. The following four conditions attempt to summarize the characteristics inherent in this process.

Meaning as formal metaphor and measurement as the mechanics of technological force both proceed from a sensible understanding of the fundamental phenomenal characteristics of gravity, climate, and sunlight.

Housing this alternate definition of natural force within the sphere of tangible human sensations defines these forces in ways that human beings might be palpably aware of. The need to do so belies an expectation about the ways in which people come to know the world around them. This expectation presupposes that the tangible world is rich ground for mental speculation. It attempts to link speculation to nature as felt force that might give rise simultaneously both to questions of quantity and to questions of emotional, intellectual, and spiritual quality.

In the Finnish log farmhouse, this application is direct and quite literal. Felt force in Orinda is a less literal matter. It is not simply the direct connection of the feltness of the natural characteristics of this force with technological form in architecture but a broader notion that feeling is conditioned by, and gives rise to, the history of human thought. Whereas the farmhouse might propose that an understanding of felt force is an innate human capacity, Orinda would propose that that feeling is, in fact, conditioned by culture as the structure of how people are able to think of issues such as those of natural force. How natural force is felt is thus an outcome, at least in part, of how it is thought about. What is important about the Wall House's stance concerning natural force as a felt phenomenon is that the core of what something is, is invested in the original act of making it. All subsequent remaking of this object is thought to carry a portion of the palpability of this original act as a necessary companion to its tangible form. And finally, Villa Savoye establishes the most rational and perhaps most abstract of these four notions of the feltness of natural force as a precondition for thinking about and manipulating that force. Nonetheless these abstractions emanate from the tangible way in which natural force is felt by human beings. Here, however, the feltness of natural force is not understood as a literal translation of the characteristics of the natural world, as a cultural interpretation of the same, or of a sense of their transcendent essence, but rather as the grounds of human reason. In this sense of the feltness of natural force, people feel as grounds for making distinctions. The ability to distinguish lies at the heart of the human capacity to attempt intellectually to understand the world through the manipulation of symbols.

Though each house treats felt natural force differently, the core of the need to do so remains intact in each of the four illustrations. If natural force were reduced to the abstractions of words or numbers in any of these instances, their particular views about the essential characteristics of natural force could not come into being. Each of these definitions speaks of technology in architecture as comprising the relationships struck by tangible form. The very notion of the tangibility of this form is premised on its ability to be felt. The possibility of it striking metaphoric relationships to the world of natural force depends equally on the ability of human beings to feel natural forces as grounds of being able to describe their surroundings. The juncture of the idea of technological form and natural force is thus initiated in each instance by the palpable qualities of each.

The mechanics of architectural responses to these forces are contained within the technological forms of buildings, but the formal meaning of technological elements is not contained in their mechanics.

This assertion establishes a nonsymmetrical relationship between mechanics and meaning in architectural technology. This asymmetry claims that technological form must always contain the mechanics inherent in the ability of these elements to empirically modify felt natural force but that those mechanics do not contain a specific form of the ensuing technological element of a building. Thus both a stone Doric column and a cylindrical steel column may support the same weight but take on a very different appearance, and therefore meaning, in doing so. It is, however, the specific form of the column in question, and not its more universal description of transmitted load, that makes a technological element a part of the design of a building.

Each of the four houses analyzed in this study comprises technological elements that perform comparable utilitarian tasks. Envelopes enclose hospitable climatic conditions from those that would prove unpleasant, frames resist gravity so that this space might be formed, and openings convey sunlight to this interiorized space so that it might be known visually and reconnected to its surroundings. To know this is to know little about the architectural qualities of the technologies employed in the four houses. Like the heat loss of a window, how each house performs these tasks can be accurately quantified. These quantities can be compared from house to house to reach numerical judgments concerning their relative technological efficiencies. But this comparison would reveal little about what each of these tools actually accomplishes in its particular setting. To understand this richer comparison requires that the form of these tools be set one against the other so that their particularities, rather than their adherence to universal measurement, might come forward.

Mechanics would demand the same, or nearly the same, resolutions to each of these technological problems. These mechanics must obviously be present to the degree necessary to prevent empirical failure, but necessary in this case is far from sufficient. The many forms that each technology assumes in each study house are clearly not simply an extension of an understanding of mechanics. These mechanical characteristics were first discovered in their material form. This form was manipulated to allow these mechanics to serve the purposes of dwelling. They were always seen, felt, and thought of as this form and not as an abstraction recited either in numbers or in words. It is these material forms that architects continue to manipulate today and not their mechanics as abstractions that may be detached from these material forms. Efforts to reduce these thoughts to empirical fact, as in the functionalism of the twentieth century, have proved not to be so much wrong as not fecund. They fail to create the kind, level, and richness of formal ideas that allow people to reside in nature.

The forms of architectural technology, therefore, carry their mechanics within them, but also so much more. They also contain the possibility of speculation about what it means to reside in a natural world. They contain the power to give birth to a never ending array of formal ideas about how this might be accomplished. They are the tangible ground on which people mount speculation concerning the significance of their existence in the natural world.

The formal meaning of technological architectural elements always explicitly manifests their instrumental origin and, hence, recalls mechanics as a condition for that meaning.

It may be less clear, having proclaimed the primary characteristic of technological form in architecture to be its metaphorical power, why this form must return to its origin as a tool as the base of its significance. Architectural design is a constrained form of the imagination. The constraint that maintains the tautness of architectural thought about technology is its need to perform empirical tasks in the natural world. Without this constraint, columns would not have to bring loads vertically to the earth. They could float as they are sometimes allowed to in a painting or a fantasy. Climate would not have to be partitioned off to create a thermal boundary, and sunlight would be allowed to appear at any time and from any direction in a building.

The ability of architectural technologies actually to modify natural force is a necessary prerequisite to their ability to take on symbolic meaning. The hearth of the Finnish log farmhouse may be a metaphor for the capacity of humankind to care for its fellows, but it would not be granted this status were it not able to store a quantity of heat. The columns of Orinda may mark a place as being of special significance to the socialization of humankind, but they could not do so had gravity not required that they be upright and permanent. The walls of the Wall House might have metaphorically separated the emptiness of a society of materialism from the insight of contemplation, but they could not have done so without the walls' tangible ability to separate climates. The horizontal openings of Villa Savoye may intellectually restate the horizon as a constructed symbol, but the power of that symbol rests squarely on the openings' ability to allow sunlight to tangibly penetrate the boundary of the house.

Tool as origin ensures that technology as a form of architectural symbol making is not capricious. The ideas that grow from the use of architectural technology are not part of an unbounded speculation that is forced to establish its own constraints. Technology as tool that complies with the dictates of empirical natural force ensures that these ideas have and always have had common ground in the notion of nature as the stable "other" inhabitant of the earth. The tool is the primary means used by the human mind to discover the order of this apparent natural stability.

The role of technology in architectural design is to present the natural world to people in a way that allows them to understand, and hence to belong within, that world.

Finally, there is the matter of why architectural technology should be considered the formation of a metaphorical understanding of nature. Nature is a unique kind of human idea. Human consciousness imagines nature to have preceded human existence, though there were no humans who could verify this assumption. It also imagines that nature will continue to exist even though we will not, an equally difficult contention to justify with any sense of certainty. This continuity of the world as nature is presented to human consciousness in nature's forms and actions. The path to understanding the nature of nature has always begun from its tangible manifestations, no matter what the outcome of these speculations have been.

A means to probe that character has been by making tools. Tools are the material and actions of nature turned on itself. Tools are only an apt means to probe the structure of nature if they are of the same basic fabric as are all nature's other activities. Within a tool is hence always the possibility of the interpretation of what constitutes nature.

Architectural technology is a special kind of tool because it locates human existence within the structure of nature. It is not an objective kind of tool that allows a detached vision of this nature because that is not the kind of issue that architecture sets out to solve. Architecture sets out to solve the issue of habitation. The architectural problem of the habitation of nature is to define its character in such a way that it might be inhabited. This is another way of saying that architectural technology need define nature in a manner that allows people to belong within it physically, emotionally, and spiritually. Architecture sees nature to be the continuous context of all things and not simply human existence within the confines of the human mind. The architectural issue of technology is thus not one of how nature belongs to us but rather one of how we belong to nature.

This notion of belonging has many ramifications. It acknowledges the articulateness of the rational frame of the Wall House and the columns that form the boundary of Villa Savoye just as it acknowledges the empirical order of the Finnish log farmhouse roof and the organization of wooden sticks that form the roof of Orinda. It acknowledges the literalness of the farmhouse's hearth as a center just as it acknowledges the abstractness of the opening in the wall around Villa Savoye as the horizon. It acknowledges the use of sunlight to name the transcendental qualities of elements that form an architectural vocabulary, as in the Wall House, just as it acknowledges the ability of openings to define the specific limits of the landscape, as in Orinda. These uses of architectural technology to define nature in ways that allow people to belong within it consist of neither a limited issue nor a mute language. Each is a means to convert the tangibe actions of the human hand into ideas that might be manipulated by the human mind. The great differences in the kinds of ideas that emanate from this hand-mind coupling are testimony to the richness of human thought, not to the "truth" concerning the structure of nature. They define the problem of how human beings are placed in nature through the things we make to inhabit.

Residence in Nature as a Perennial Architectural Problem

Human beings have always developed metaphorical thought concerning events of life that are important to them. There are few, if any, subjects of human intercourse that have not been found by the human mind to be worthy of speculation about their real, underlying, or essential characteristics. It seems that people are simply unable to take the world the way they find it. They suffer from a compulsion to make of the world a structure of ideas, of speculation about the underlying meaning of the things that share life with them. It would be strange, then, if the foremost of earthly human companions, nature, did not share in this kind of idea making.

It became intellectually popular in late-nineteenth-century science to strip nature of its metaphoric potential to do so. A totally literal definition of nature emerged under the rubric of empiricism as a function of numerical symbols and of literal thought. The science of this period flowered under a seemingly endless stream of successes that appeared to give credence to the concept that all in the natural world might be reduced to ideas that stemmed from a quantitative understanding of mass and energy. Banishing metaphorical thought concerning the underlying structure of the ideas of nature was seen to be "the ascent of man." Nature was effectively placed outside the boundaries of metaphorical thought by this assertion.

Today there remains an enormous inertia to a mechanical vision of technology that argues against all other interpretations of its significance. Things that work well are held in high esteem in our culture. That which requires interpretation to divulge its significance is suspect. In *The Gutenberg Elegies,* Sven Birkerts contends that we are willing to trade the private intellectual space of reading for the look-alike, faster, flashier, more transparent, but intellectually less satisfying screen of the computer monitor in the name of technological progress. But like Birkerts's plea for the unmeasurable pleasures of reading a book, there is a sense of loss that follows each of us in this fast-paced era of technological innovation and invasion of our lives. Some would call this sense of loss nostalgia. To them, people who do not welcome contemporary definitions of technological progress are Luddites: small-minded individuals who are simply unable to keep up with the rate of technological change that is supposed to characterize modernity. To the rest of us, however, there is something more to this loss. It is defined in Michael Benedikt's discussion of an "architecture of reality"; it is Birkerts's lamenting the loss of the intellectual privacy of reading; it is our own sense of the distance that machines and electronic devices create in our lives when we are at a seashore or in the light of the forest. This sense of loss does not argue that an empirical definition of nature, with its attendant need for measurement, does not exist or is untrue. Nor is the abstract definition of this empiricism in mathematics that characterizes modern science being questioned. Rather, it is the tyranny of a purely mechanical vision of nature that is inherent in science and engineering that our sense of loss suggests should be scrutinized more carefully in deliberations concerning technology.

But technology in architecture is not the product of scientific thought. It has benefited from the numerous discoveries of modern science, but in the final analysis, it clings to a much more primitive and immediate definition of nature than is evidenced in the abstractions of mathematics. The four houses of this study illustrate the kind of nature that architectural technology gives birth to as metaphorical thought. These four houses certainly do not present an exhaustive list of the metaphorical natures that emanate from architectural technology. They do, however, open up the possibility of such definitions as the unique and critical characteristic of architecture's technological voice.

There remain few dedicated positivists at the end of the twentieth century. What attitudes should replace the positivism of the early part of the century seem to be in doubt. Perhaps architecture is an apt vocabulary and set of issues to shed some light on this dilemma. Because it has never been able to avoid the problem of not working empirically as a tool in an unchanging world of natural force, architecture has never, as a discipline, been able to escape the tenets of empiricism. Because these tools have always been located in material forms, the discipline of architecture has always had to deal with the problem that symbolic ideas would become attached to these forms. Because these were forms that people would inhabit, architecture has never been able to avoid the problem that the symbolic ideas people attach to these forms will be about their own existence. There is then a long and continuous history of how architecture has attempted to rectify ideas of empiricism with those of symbolic meanings throughout time. This has been a search not of choice but of necessity. The issue of architecture as a place to dwell would not allow otherwise.

Most of us will probably continue to read books even in a computer age exactly because of the private intellectual space that Birkerts so beautifully writes about. There is an architecture of the real that Benedikt so insightfully searches for because people remain concerned about what "real" really is. Building technologies like a window on a winter morning do speak to us at other levels than can be defined by utility and performance. We do care that they effectively perform empirical tasks, but we also care what they feel like. We care about why they are significant events in our lives. We care that we are, in some measure, responsible for them and they for us. We care about what they say about us and our culture. In short, we care about what they mean as well as about how well they perform.

Select Bibliography

Allen, Edward. *Fundamentals of Building Construction*. New York: John Wiley and Sons, 1990.

Bachelard, Gaston. *The Poetics of Space*. Boston: Beacon Press, 1964.

———. *The Psychoanalysis of Fire*. Boston: Beacon Press, 1969.

Banham, Reyner. *The Architecture of the Well-Tempered Environment*. London: Architectural Press; Chicago: University of Chicago Press, 1969.

Benedikt, Michael. *For an Architecture of Reality*. New York: Lumen Books, 1987.

Billington, David P. *The Tower and the Bridge*. Princeton, N.J.: Princeton University Press, 1983.

Birkerts, Sven. *The Gutenberg Elegies: The Fate of Reading in the Electronic Age*. New York: Fawcett Columbine, 1995.

Bloomer, Kent C., and Charles W. Moore. *Body, Memory, and Architecture*. New Haven: Yale University Press, 1977.

Bognar, Botond. *Contemporary Japanese Architecture*. New York: Van Nostrand Reinhold, 1985.

Bronowski, Jacob. *The Ascent of Man*. Boston: Little Brown, 1973.

Brown, G. Z., Bruce Haglund, John Reynolds, Joel Loveland, and Susan Ubbelohde. *Inside Out*. New York: John Wiley and Sons, 1992.

Colquhoun, Alan. *Modernity and the Classical Tradition*. Cambridge: MIT Press, 1989.

Commoner, Barry. *The Closing Circle: Nature, Man, and Technology*. New York: Knopf, 1971.

Elliot, Cecil D. *Technics and Architecture*. Cambridge: MIT Press, 1992.

Ellul, Jacques. *The Technological Society*. New York: Alfred A. Knopf, 1967.

Fitch, Marston. *American Building*. New York: Houghton Mifflin, 1972.

Fuller, Buckminster. *Ideas and Integrities*. New York: Macmillan, 1963.

Gropius, Walter, Kenzo Tange, Yasuhiro Ishimoto, and Herbert Bayer. *Katsura Tradition and Creation in Japanese Architecture*. New Haven: Yale University Press, 1960.

Hajdu, Peter. *Finno-Ugrian Languages and Peoples*. London: Andre Deutsch, 1975.

Hawkes, Jacquetta. *The Atlas of Early Man*. New York: St. Martin's Press, 1976.

Heidegger, Martin. *Poetry, Language, Thought*. New York: Harper Colophon Books, 1975.

Herdeg, Klaus. *The Decorated Diagram*. Cambridge: MIT Press, 1983.

Hofstadter, Albert, and Thomas Kuhns. *Philosophies of Art and Beauty*. Chicago: University of Chicago Press, 1964.

Hurtt, Steven W. "Le Corbusier: Type, Archetype, and Iconography." In *Type and the (Im)possibilities of Convention*, ed. Garth Rockcastle. New York: Princeton Architectural Press, 1991.

Kepes, Gyorgy. *The Man-Made Object*. New York: George Braziller, 1966.

Koestler, Arthur. *The Watershed*. New York: Anchor Books Doubleday, 1960.

Kolehmainen, Alfred, and Valokuvat Veijo A. Laine. *Suomalainen talonpoikaistalo*. Keuruu: Kustannusokakeyhtiö Otava painolaitokset, 1980.

Kranzberg, Melvin, and Carroll W. Pursell, eds. *Technology in Western Civilization*. New York: Oxford University Press, 1967.

Kuhn, Thomas S. *The Copernican Revolution*. Cambridge: Harvard University Press, 1957.

———. *The Structure of Scientific Revolutions*. Chicago: University of Chicago Press, 1970.

Langer, Susanne K. *Feeling and Form*. New York: Charles Scribner and Sons, 1953.

———. *Philosophy in a New Key: A Study in the Symbolism of Reason, Rite, and Art*. Cambridge: Harvard University Press, 1957.

Lechner, Norbert. *Heating, Cooling, Lighting*. John Wiley and Sons, 1991.

Le Corbusier. *Toward a New Architecture*. London: Architectural Press, 1959.

Mazria, Edward. *The Passive Solar Energy Book*. Emmaus, Pa.: Rodale Press, 1979.

McCleary, Peter. "Some Characteristics of a New Concept of Technology." *Journal of Architectural Education* 42, no. 1 (1988): 4–9.

Mead, W. R., and Helmer Smeds. *Winter in Finland*. London: Hugh Evelyn, 1967.

Merritt, Raymond H. *Engineering in American Society, 1850–1875*. Lexington: University Press of Kentucky, 1969.

Moore, Charles Willard. *Place of Houses*. New York: Holt, Rinehart and Winston, 1974.

Moore, Fuller. *Concepts and Practice of Architectural Daylighting*. New York: Van Nostrand Reinhold, 1991.

Mumford, Lewis. *Roots of Contemporary American Architecture*. New York: Reinhold, 1952.

Norberg-Shulz, Christian. *Intentions in Architecture*. Cambridge: MIT Press, 1965.

———. *Towards a Phenomenology of Architecture*. New York: Rizzoli, 1979.

Ortega y Gasset, José. *Toward a Philosophy of History*. New York: W. W. Norton, 1941.

Pardo, Vittorio Franchetti. *Le Corbusier: The Life and Work of the Artist Illustrated with Eighty Color Plates*. London: Thames and Hudson, 1971.

Platt, Raye R., ed. *Finland and Its Geography: An American Geographical Society Handbook*. New York: Duell, Sloan and Pearce, 1955.

Rapoport, Amos. *House, Form, and Culture.* Englewood Cliffs, N.J.: Prentice Hall, 1969.

Read, Herbert. "The Origin of Art as Form." In *The Man-Made Object,* ed. Gyorgy Kepes. New York: G. Braziller, 1960.

Reischauer, Edwin O. *The Japanese Today.* Tokyo: Charles E. Tuttle, 1977.

Rowe, Colin. *The Mathematics of the Ideal Villa and Other Essays.* Cambridge: MIT Press, 1990.

Ruskin, John. *Seven Lamps of Architecture.* New York: Harper, 1900.

Rykwert, Joseph. *On Adam's House in Paradise.* Cambridge: MIT Press, 1981.

Slavson, David A. *Secret Teachings in the Art of Japanese Gardens.* Tokyo: Kodansha International, 1991.

Snow, C. P. *The Two Cultures.* Cambridge: Cambridge University Press, 1980.

Snyder, Robert. *Buckminster Fuller.* New York: St. Martin's Press, 1980.

Whitehead, Alfred North. *Science and the Modern World.* New York: New American Library, 1925.

Index

Lance LaVine is professor of architecture at the University of Minnesota. He is the author of *Five Degrees of Conservation*, as well as numerous articles that address the role of technology in architecture.